W9-CGQ-979

FOOD X FIRE

GRILLING AND BBQ WITH

DEREK WOLF

OVER THE FIRE
COOKING

HARVARD
COMMON
PRESS

JUL - - 2021

To my parents, Brad and Denise Wolf,

who diligently paved the way for me, this business, and my family.

May you see a double share of favor because of your love.

Inspiring | Educating | Creating | Entertaining

Brimming with creative inspiration, how-to projects, and useful information to enrich your everyday life, Quarto Knows is a favorite destination for those pursuing their interests and passions. Visit our site and dig deeper with our books into your area of interest: Quarto Creates, Quarto Cooks, Quarto Homes, Quarto Lives, Quarto Drives, Quarto Explores, Quarto Gifts, or Quarto Kids.

© 2021 Quarto Publishing Group USA Inc.
Text © 2020 Derek Wolf
Photography © 2020 <if required>

First Published in 2021 by The Harvard Common Press, an imprint of The Quarto Group, 100 Cummings Center, Suite 265-D, Beverly, MA 01915, USA.
T (978) 282-9590 F (978) 283-2742 QuartoKnows.com

All rights reserved. No part of this book may be reproduced in any form without written permission of the copyright owners. All images in this book have been reproduced with the knowledge and prior consent of the artists concerned, and no responsibility is accepted by producer, publisher, or printer for any infringement of copyright or otherwise, arising from the contents of this publication. Every effort has been made to ensure that credits accurately comply with information supplied. We apologize for any inaccuracies that may have occurred and will resolve inaccurate or missing information in a subsequent reprinting of the book.

The Harvard Common Press titles are also available at discount for retail, wholesale, promotional, and bulk purchase. For details, contact the Special Sales Manager by email at specialsales@quarto.com or by mail at The Quarto Group, Attn: Special Sales Manager, 100 Cummings Center, Suite 265-D, Beverly, MA 01915, USA.

25 24 23 22 21   3 4 5 6 7

ISBN: 978-1-59233-975-4

Digital edition published in 2021

Library of Congress Control Number: 2021930243

Cover Design: Tanya Jacobson, jcbsn.co
Interior Design and Page Layout: Allison Meierding
Photography: Jack Sorokin Photography

Printed in Canada

CONTENTS

———

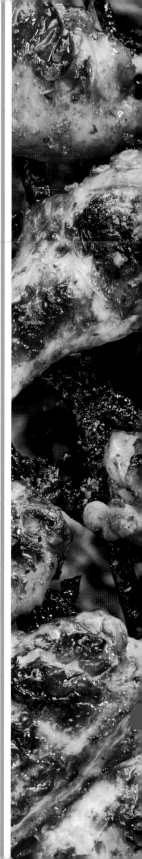

177 | CHAPTER 5 | SAUCES, MARINADES, AND RUBS

INTRODUCTION

—

If I am honest, my fire cooking journey started while watching television, procrastinating on schoolwork. Yes, I know that sounds ridiculous, but I fell in love with the idea that you could cook more than just hot dogs and hamburgers on a campfire. This style of cooking is so rustic and natural it is almost purely human.

HOW IT ALL STARTED

After watching the South American Chef Francis Mallmann show the world the depths of fire cooking, I found myself thinking, "Maybe I could do this at home?" My wife and I got a firepit and a DSLR camera as wedding presents a couple months later. While feeling stuck and uninspired by my corporate job, I decided to take a stab at cooking skirt steak over the open flames.

I went to an outdoor shop and bought a simple "pop-over" grill that we placed on our firepit. I made skirt steak with a crude chimichurri sauce. I was hooked. The smell of the smoke and flames wafting in the air as the steak sizzled was enough to make a grown man cry. Well, at least make a grown man hungry . . . I decided that night that, if I were cooking, it would be over fire.

I started cooking all kinds of food over open flames, trying to absorb as much knowledge as I could. In the early days, I bought two of everything to cook because I knew I would burn, undercook, or destroy the first attempt.

While I was cooking, my wife started taking photos. She encouraged me to start a social media page about my fire cooking journey. I was hesitant because I truly did not love social media. Finally, after a few weeks of persistence, I started the page *Over The Fire Cooking*. It was hit.

OVER THE FIRE COOKING

Well, maybe not an overnight hit, but we grew like crazy on Instagram. At first, I just wanted to showcase chefs and cooks that inspired me to cook over open flames. People fell in love with the mission of bringing fire, food, and people together. Soon thereafter, people wanted my recipes and photos to be center stage. I took the leap and started writing recipes, articles, and cooking tips from the lessons I learned along my journey.

It is always a scary moment when you make something yourself, knowing full well that people could love it, hate it, or straight up despise it. Even with the turmoil and judgment you find on social media, I took the leap.

After a couple months showcasing my recipes, people were hooked! We started a blog and all the other social media, so everyone could join our journey. Slowly but surely, my knowledge for cooking grew to a point where I could no longer just keep it online. I wanted to expand—thus began the arduous process of writing a cookbook.

This cookbook is the memoir of my successes and failures. It is the flavor of those that have shown me grace when I was undeserving and mercy when I knew fully that I needed to be better. It is the testimony that anyone can learn to cook, grow, and love when others invest in you.

Every recipe, sauce, seasoning, and flavor in this book tells a story of a young kid who fell in love with the idea that food is more than just food . . .

FIRE, FOOD, AND PEOPLE

"Food is more than just food"—one of my favorite things to say when people ask why I cook over fire. Why?

The truth is, we all want to belong. We all want a sense of identity that is both easy to understand, yet complex enough to be unique. There are many avenues that produce this level of self— and food is the path I chose.

Whether you grew up in the Southeastern United States, like I did, or somewhere else far away, food brings people together. It is a symbol of unity, understanding, and acceptance. It is a place of comfort when we feel overwhelmed and an offering of peace when we are in the wrong.

It is a quintessential piece of life that nourishes a part of our inner core: our sense of community. That said, there is no better example than food cooked over fire.

Cooking with fire is one of the few things that makes us human. Everywhere you go in the world, you find traditional recipes using similar ingredients for the same purpose: feeding the ones we love. When it takes 8 to 12 hours to cook something over the flames, you are doing it for more than just fun. You are doing it to share the experience with others. When I cook over fire, it is because I am on a journey to bring fire, food, and people together.

Through recipes like Whole Lamb al Asador (page 109) or Herb Brush-Basted Bone-In Rib Eye (page 49), you will discover delicious food made to be shared. These are meals that encourage you to invite guests. They are meals to make for those like you—and those who are not. They will push you with flavors inspired from far parts of the world or twists on dishes closer to home.

So, in this book, may you learn that food is more than just food but also an expression of love. May you fall in love with cooking over fire, with all its nuances and successes. Finally, may you learn that cooking over fire not only brings us together but, perhaps, might show us we are not that different to begin with.

1
GETTING STARTED: RESPECTING THE FLAME

While growing up, my dad would tell me surfing stories from his childhood. He described days spent driving up and down the California Coast, searching for that "perfect wave." Every once in a while, he would catch that wave. He said, in those moments, it was almost like time stopped—and he was in unison with something that was more than just a wave. It was something . . . uncontrollable.

This is what I feel when I am cooking over fire.

Cooking with fire is not about fancy grills, expensive meat, or crazy recipes. It has been, and always will be, about learning to work with something not fully controllable: fire. No, I am not talking about the science and chemistry of fire. I am underqualified to even attempt that conversation (though it's flattering if you thought that's what I meant). I am talking about how fire is unpredictable, unwavering, and uninterested in doing what you tell it to do.

Just like a living being, fire will go where it wants to go and do what it wants to do—all while giving off its two most valuable assets—heat and light. That is why I always err on the side of respecting the flame.

I don't mean you need to be afraid of fire or pretend it is some immortal object. What I do mean is you need to be aware that, like humanity, fire is not tamable. You can work with it, understand it, and try to find common ground, but in the end, the fire will always take its own path. Respecting the flame means learning to see and hear its cues and signals while still understanding it is a powerful tool not for the faint of heart. Let's get acquainted with the tools and techniques you'll need.

DANCING WITH FIRE

Fire is one of the greatest assets humanity has ever worked with but we must treat it with respect. Understanding that it will not immediately do exactly what you want it to do is the beauty of cooking with fire. The best you can do is learn to understand fire. It is like a dance. By following its lead, fire cooking will teach you patience, intuition, and adaptability.

While cooking my recipes, you will find yourself rekindling a dying fire, taming one that's out of control, or even feeling stuck before getting started—struggling to get a spark. When you feel that way, just know we have all been there. (Keeping me accountable, my wife can attest to the number of cooks I have ruined because of too little fire, too much fire, or no fire at all.) Every painstaking step it has taken to learn to master fire cooking, I have walked. The best part is, I feel I have not mastered it all and have many more dance steps to learn!

Whether you have explored fire cooking before or this is the first time, I want you to succeed with minimal frustration. Here, and in the recipes, I give you every tip and trick I have learned. May you conquer any frustrations and soon be as infatuated with fire cooking as I was when I discovered it. It is my hope that fire cooking might even teach you more than how to cook a specific recipe—whether that means mastering a new tool or technique or learning to appreciate the company around the fire.

The Two Types of Fire Cooking

Let's kick things off by breaking down the world of fire cooking. There are many styles and various devices used to cook over fire, but there are only two main ways to use the heat from fire to cook your food: *directly* and *indirectly*. Picking one of these two fire cooking methods determines how the food will be cooked, what devices will be used, and the overall flavor of the food.

DIRECT FIRE COOKING   Direct fire cooking, in my definition, is the process of cooking directly over heat created by the wood or coals from the fire. Since you are cooking close to the embers, you can get a good char, caramelization, and strong wood flavor into your food. This cooking style tends to favor thinner, less fatty cuts of meat, as it relies on speed to get the food cooked. (If a cut of meat is too thick, it can be hard to get the proper level of doneness inside by the time the outside is where you want it.) Cuts like skirt steak, bacon, and chicken wings are staples in my direct cooking repertoire. That said, I am not shy when it comes to trying delicate foods over the flame. I love cooking eggs in cast iron, searing scallops, and grilling shrimp with direct heat. Direct heat cooking is very versatile, which is why it is the most widely used style of fire cooking in the world.

INDIRECT FIRE COOKING   Indirect fire cooking, by my definition, is the process of cooking near or around the fire using its weaker radiant heat. This is the cooking style that makes brisket, rotisserie chicken, and lamb *al Asador* possible. Indirect cooking tends to be best with fattier, thicker, and more delicate cuts of meat you want cooked away from the harshness of the fire's direct heat. Indirect cooking, while slower, will prevent burning and open the door to breaking down intermuscular fat. This creates much more tender meat, as the fat will no longer be chewy but, rather, melt into the meat itself. Overall, it is a great way to cook densely fat cuts.

In the end, learning to utilize direct and indirect cooking will help you master fire cooking itself. We'll dive deeper into the types of cooking you can do with each style starting on page 27. But first, let's look at gear and techniques you'll need no matter how you cook with fire.

The Basic Gear

The funny part about gear is that most fire cooking does not require a ton of it. In fact, if you have hot coals and tongs, you don't even need a grill. However, there's no reason to make cooks harder than they need to be. Here are some essentials I couldn't do without.

Portable grill: I have a couple different portable grills I use, but more than a specific brand, I highly recommend something lightweight that is easy to throw in the back of your car. Pop-over grills, simple grills ready to be placed over the fire, such as a grill grate with legs to stand over the flames, or a swivel grill grate you hammer into the ground, tend to be my favorite, but there are numerous grills on the market made exactly for this ready-to-use-anywhere purpose.

Pitchfork: I use a traditional metal pitchfork, along with my fire-resistant gloves (see following) for moving coals. The pitchfork can be found at most outdoor or garden shops. It is ideal for picking up hot logs or breaking apart a lit fire.

Cast-iron skillet: I never leave my house to cook without my cast-iron skillet. I have been using the same 12-inch (30 cm) skillet since the beginning of my journey and will continue to use it for life. Although cast iron might be heavy, it is versatile. Make sure to read the section on how to clean it properly (see page 66) because keeping a good seasoning on the skillet is key.

Natural fire starters and matches: These are key to fire cooking because if you can't get a fire going, you won't be cooking at all. I recommend natural tumbleweed-style fire starters instead of lighter fluid or something synthetic. You want your food to taste like the wood and smoke from the fire, not the lighter fluid.

Fire-resistant gloves: Using gloves while cooking over fire is essential. This will help prevent burns as well as other mishaps. I use my gloves for picking up hot cast iron, moving grates, or placing new logs to the fire. I buy barbecue gloves from home and garden stores because they are made to last. Look for good-quality leather gloves built for high heat. Also, before you're in the heat of a cook, check that they are heat/fire "resistant." You don't want to find out they're not when pulling your hot cast iron off the fire one day (speaking from experience).

Sharp axe: Every fire cook needs a sharp axe for splitting wood. There's nothing wrong with buying a nice axe either, like cast iron; they can last for years.

Thermometer: You will need reliable thermometers when cooking with fire to measure internal temperature of foods as they cook. See page 19 for more information.

Cooking tools: My cooking tools bag usually includes a sharp knife, cutting board (wood or synthetic), tongs, and a wooden spatula. Why wooden? It is heat resistant and won't scratch your skillets when stirring.

Checking Internal Temperature

In my recipes, I often recommend a specific internal temperature to gauge doneness. At first, you might be tempted to overlook this information, but I assure you it is important to making delicious, properly cooked foods. For those who like medium-rare steaks versus medium steaks, you do not need to rely on luck to get your steaks done right. For those who tend to overcook chicken to be on the "safe side," there is a proper internal temperature that allows you to know when it is safe to consume—and not burned or dry.

PROBING WITH A THERMOMETER You will need a thermometer to check internal temperatures of the food you're cooking. I prefer a digital thermometer, but any food-safe thermometer that is properly calibrated will work for checking the temperature of most meats.

When checking the meat, insert the thermometer into the middle of the thickest part of the meat, without touching any bone, so you understand how hot the food really is. When the thermometer touches the bone, it most often reads at a higher temperature than is accurate. The meat close to the bone will inversely read at temperatures lower than accurate. If you place the thermometer on the outside layers of the food, you might get a higher reading than expected because the heat cooks the outside of the food faster than the inside.

I find the thickest part of the meat and place my thermometer in the middle there as it will give me the most accurate temperature reading possible. For steaks, I like placing the thermometer in the widest part of the meat. For chicken, I like to place it in the middle of the breast to get an accurate read. Whatever you do, as noted earlier, avoid touching a bone with the thermometer. This throws off your reading and gives you an inaccurate internal temperature.

CARRYOVER COOKING AND LETTING MEAT REST Before I move on to the specifics of internal temperature, I want to discuss the idea of carryover cooking and letting meat rest before cutting it. While cooking your meat, you will be tempted to do two things: cook the meat all the way until it hits the ideal internal temperature and cut into your food right after pulling it off the fire. These are not ideal ways to cook.

With regard to cooking meat until it hits its ideal internal temperature, many people do not realize that food continues to cook even after you pull it off the fire. The meat is still hot from the fire and will carry over (hence the name "carryover cooking") the heat from the grill. So, what was a medium-rare steak at 125°F (52°C) on the grill will continue to cook for the next 3 to 5 minutes, when it will end up being a medium steak at 130°F (54°C) once rested. If you were shooting for a medium steak, that would be perfect. However, if you wanted a nice medium-rare, then you just overcooked your steak. To prevent this, pull the meat off the fire about 5°F to 10°F (3°C to 6°C), depending on the cut of meat, less than your ideal temperature and let the carryover heat slowly rise to the ideal internal temperature.

This is related to my other point: I believe it's important to let cooked meat rest. By slightly undercooking your food, then allowing it to rest, the heat in the meat evens out and does not overcook your food as the temperature continues to rise. I've also found the juices often seem more evenly distributed in the meat after letting it rest. There has been some work in the food science arena debating the value of resting versus slicing right away. Because it is an ongoing discussion, your belief may be different from mine. That's okay! If you want to follow the advice to let it rest, let's discuss how to do it.

HOW TO REST COOKED MEAT   Okay, the previous section has you sold. But how do you rest meat properly? To avoid temptation, I cover the meat with aluminum foil and place it on a counter that's out of the way, in a room-temperature cooler, or an unheated oven. The insulation from the foil, cooler, or oven will help keep the food from going cold while resting. An out-of-the-way location will also help keep you from changing your mind and serving the food too early.

It's also key to let the meat rest for the proper amount of time. Whereas a normal rib eye or pork chop might need only 5 to 7 minutes to rest, larger pieces of meat, like a prime rib or leg of lamb, can require 30 to 40 minutes to rest. By giving the meat the proper time, you end up with the best quality dinner with superior texture and flavor. Just build in that rest time when planning your cook.

Internal Temperature for Meats

Here is a quick glance at the ideal internal temperatures for your food, after resting:

Beef: See breakdown on page 21
Chicken: minimum 165°F (74°C)
Pork: minimum 145°F (63°C), however
        some cuts like ribs or shoulder will cook
        into the 200°Fs (about 90°C to 100°Cs)
        to break down more of the fat
Fish and Seafood: 145°F (63°C)
Ground Meat: minimum 160°F (71°C)

Beef Internal Temperature	
There are tons of variations on which temperature ranges equate to rare, medium-rare, and steak temperatures in general. These guidelines are what I follow for internal temperature on steaks—after resting:	
Blue	100°F to 110°F (38°C to 43°C)
Rare	110°F to 120°F (43°C to 49°C)
Medium-rare	120°F to 130°F (49°C to 54°C)
Medium	130°F to 140°F (54°C to 60°C)
Well-done	140°F+ (60°C+)
Note: USDA recommends a minimum internal temperature of 145°F (63°C) for beef (not ground).	

DONENESS TEST FOR STEAK   If you ever find yourself without a working thermometer, you can check the internal temperature of steak using your hand. Although this is only an approximation and not a perfectly accurate way of testing internal temperature of steaks, it is always a fun party trick to impress friends or fellow fire cooks.

1.   Hold out one hand, palm up, unclenched and relaxed. Using your pointer finger of the opposite hand, gently press on your open palm at the base of your thumb. Your palm will be relatively easy to press into, as the muscle is not tight.

2.   With your open hand, flex your pointer finger toward your palm and, using the pointer finger of your opposite had, press on the same spot. It is a bit firmer. Now, flex your middle finger toward your palm and do the same thing, pressing into the palm of your hand, and so on. The palm gradually becomes more tense and less forgiving.

3.   Each finger corresponds to the internal temperature of the steak when pressed. When checking the steak, the meat should have the same tension or lack of tension. Here is a breakdown:

Rare	Opposite pointer finger pressing on unclenched, relaxed palm
Medium-rare	Pointer finger of open hand flexed toward palm, touching palm with opposite pointer finger
Medium	Middle finger flexed toward palm
Medium-well	Ring finger flexed toward palm
Well-done	Pinky finger flexed toward palm

Fire Temperature and the Hand Test

One of the biggest keys to cooking is understanding the temperature of the fire. Whether doing a hot sear or a slow smoke, understanding the heat will help you make better decisions when cooking. You can rely on the temperature gauge on the outside of your grill . . . but a campfire does not have a temperature gauge—so, how do you check the heat?

You can get a good idea of how hot a fire is with your hand. **Be careful**: fire can be hotter than

you think—even at a distance. Proceed slowly and only do this if you can keep your hand safe from the fire you are trying to gauge. Starting farther away, slowly move in until you are holding your hand about 4 inches (10 cm) from the fire. Once at this target distance, use a stopwatch to measure, in seconds, how long you can hold your hand there without needing to pull it away because it is uncomfortable (not painful). The time you measure will give you a good sense on how hot the fire is. Again, respect that fire and understand it can be very hot (speaking from experience).

	Temperature	Hand test	Cooking styles
Low	200°F to 250°F (93°C to 120°C)	10 to 12 seconds	Barbecue
Medium-Low	250°F to 300°F (120°C to 150°C)	8 to 10 seconds	Barbecue, Hanging, Leaning, Rotisserie
Medium	300°F to 350°F (150°C to 180°C)	6 to 8 seconds	Grilling, Hanging, Leaning, Skewers/ Rotisserie, Skillet
Medium-High	350°F to 400°F (180°C to 200°C)	4 to 5 seconds	Grilling, Skewers/ Rotisserie, Skillet
High	400°F+ (200°C+)	2 to 3 seconds	Grilling

Using Good Wood

Great ingredients are the key to great cooking, and for fire cooking, wood is a key ingredient. No matter how good a cook you are, using water-logged wood to start a hot fire is not ideal. I recommend using well-seasoned hardwoods for cooking. That means getting wood that has been eradicated of moisture and resin so you have a super-hot fire that is not popping and smoking the whole time. Another great alternative is lump charcoal, which we will discuss later (see page 24).

Good seasoned wood can be found online, but I prefer to buy it locally from farmers or ranchers. This wood tends to be kept well and it keeps money in my community. Local home and garden stores often stock seasoned wood most of the year as well.

TYPES OF WOOD AND WHAT TO COOK WITH THEM There are many different species and types of wood. Not all make good fire-cooking wood, though. Some local seasoned hardwoods I use most for cooking are cherry, hickory, and oak. Hardwoods like these tend to burn longer with higher intensity and great smoke flavor compared to softwoods. Even wood chunks or wood chips made from these woods can be great alternatives if you struggle to find larger pieces of wood.

While those woods are what I source most in my area, there are many more types of hardwoods out there. All create different flavor profiles on the food, but not all types of hardwoods create flavors that go well with all types of meat. Here is a quick breakdown of some common hardwoods and their food pairings for cooking over fire.

Wood type	Character	Meats
Alder	Light and Earthy	Seafood, Vegetables
Apple	Mild and Sweet	Chicken, Pork, Seafood
Cherry	Mild and Fruity	Chicken, Lamb, Pork, Seafood
Hickory	Strong and Smoky	Beef, Pork
Mesquite	Strong and Spicy	Beef, Lamb, Pork
Oak	Strong and Versatile	Beef, Chicken, Lamb, Pork, Seafood
Pecan	Light and Smoky	Beef, Chicken, Pork, Vegetables

Lump Charcoal and Charcoal Chimneys

While I tend to use real wood more often when fire cooking, I do love the flavor lump charcoal provides. Lump charcoal, if you're unfamiliar with it, is real wood that has been burned until all the chemicals and moisture from the wood are eradicated. Once processed, it is broken into small coals and sold for cooking. It is a great source of heat, and all it takes to get started is some natural fire starters and a charcoal chimney.

Charcoal chimneys are vertical cylinders with a handle on the side. The chimney helps get the coals hot, while providing a method to dump the coals onto the fires so you can use them for cooking. Here is how you start a fire using a charcoal chimney:

1. Fill the charcoal chimney with lump charcoal. The amount of heat you need will determine how full you fill the chimney. One full charcoal chimney will give off a medium-high to high temperature, perfect for direct cooking. A three-fourths-full chimney provides a good medium temperature, ideal for some direct-style cooking and indirect cooking. A half-full chimney is great for low- to medium-low-temperature cooking.

   For grills with large surface areas, use two chimneys to get a high heat.

   Plus, add wood chips or wood chunks to the coals for added smoke flavor and to control the temperature.

2. Place the chimney on a fire-resistant surface or inside your unlit grill.

3. Place some newspaper (no glossy or colored pages, though), or natural fire starters, such as tumbleweed, underneath the chimney and light it. I use two fire starters to start a full charcoal chimney and three to start my fires. Natural fire starters are quick to light and do not give off any odor or smell to the coals or food.

4. Let the chimney burn until most of the coals at the top of the chimney are glowing red-hot.

5. When ready to use the charcoal, wear heat-resistant gloves when handling the chimney as it will be very warm. Dump the coals into your grill, or onto the fire, as needed.

DIRECT FIRE COOKING

Whether it was hot dogs over the campfire or a burger on the backyard grill, you probably have some experience with food charred over a hot flame. Direct cooking is as simple as placing a piece of food over hot coals and letting it cook. Every once in a while, you might need to flip the food; when it is done, pull it off the fire. The same premise is the foundation of the following three subsections: Grilling, Skillet, and Cooking on the Coals.

Grilling involves cooking on a grill grate placed close over the coals. Skillet cooking is done in a cast-iron or metal pan used for direct cooking over the heat. Cooking on coals is exactly as described! All three styles of cooking make for a fun and fascinating exploration of fire cooking. However, all three require different fire-building techniques, equipment, and wood. Let's look more closely at each.

Grilling

RECIPES START ON PAGE 47.

Description: Grilling is a fast-paced, high-heat cooking style that relies on hot metal grates. These metal grates hold the food above the flame, and allow some smoke and flavor from the wood to kiss the outside of the meat. Some meats well-suited for the grill include chicken wings, pork chops, and rib eyes.

How to build the fire: Building a fire for grilling is straightforward using the "log cabin" technique—arranging wood logs on top of each other, creating a square structure with wood shavings between each log. The shavings help the fire catch quickly so you can make the "core," or center, of the fire super-hot. If the core stays hot, your fire will continue burning at a consistent temperature for the duration of your cook. This is a great fire for grilling because it creates heat that goes directly up instead of out. When it comes to cooking, we want a fire that maintains an even temperature over a flat surface. Most fires have cool spots and hot spots. With a log cabin set-up, the fire burns at a relatively equal rate while giving you a large surface area to cook over. All this means we can begin cooking knowing things will cook at the same rate without the fire burning the food or drying it out.

1. Begin by splitting logs into 10 to 12 (2-inch, or 5 cm-thick) pieces. Aim for a range of width in the pieces, with the most important pieces being the thin shavings.

2. In a safely enclosed grilling area, like a fire ring or fire pit, lay 2 pieces of wood parallel to each other, about 2 to 3 inches (5 to 7.5 cm) apart. Place your natural fire starters in the middle of the 2 logs and light them.

3. Build another layer on top with 2 similarly sized pieces, perpendicular to the logs under them. Between the second layer of logs, add 1 or 2 thin slices of wood that will catch very easily.

4. Continue building layers, repeating step 3, until you have 4 to 6 layers. Let the fire burn naturally for 30 to 40 minutes.

5. Once the wood pieces begin to split from burning, push the pile close together. Begin checking the fire for your desired cooking temperature.

6. When it is within the temperature for your cook, add a grill grate to preheat for 2 to 3 minutes.

7. Begin cooking! As your wood begins to break down, place more 2-inch (5 cm) logs or lump charcoal on top to maintain the temperature.

Special equipment: You'll just need the basic gear list on page 16.

Skillet

RECIPES START ON PAGE 63.

Description: Cooking in a cast-iron skillet is one of the best ways to diversify your direct cooking experience. Working with cast iron is a great way to learn how to control temperature, as you do not want the skillet to be super-hot. There are many delicious recipes we will explore with this cooking style—from eggs to scallops.

How to build the fire: Building a fire for skillet cooking is similar to that for grilling, with a few tweaks. You will want to elevate the skillet above the fire instead of placing it right on the coals. This will help the fire stay hot longer instead of being smothered by the skillet.

1. Follow steps 1 through 4 on page 29.

5. As the coals (broken down logs in your burning wood pile) break down, push the logs away from the center and place your cast-iron stand, or iron grate, in the middle. Carefully build up the logs again around the base of the stand. Start to check the fire for your desired cooking temperature.

6. Once the fire is ready, place the skillet on the stand over the fire for 2 to 3 minutes to preheat before cooking.

7. Begin cooking. As the wood breaks down, place more logs under the skillet to maintain the temperature. Remember to keep a good airflow underneath the skillet for optimal heat.

Special equipment: In addition to a quality cast-iron skillet—one that can withstand the high intensity of fire cooking!—grab a well-built skillet cooking stand, as it helps keep airflow going in the fire, so the coals can still "breathe" while giving off heat. If you do not have a skillet stand, use a grill grate. I prefer the skillet stand because you can build the fire around it, which creates a longer, hotter burn.

Cooking on the Coals

RECIPES START ON PAGE 80.

Description: Cooking foods directly on coals is an absolute blast—and it transfers delicious flavor to your food. I've found that when cooking on the coals, it's best to wait for the coals to become white-hot. Once they are extremely hot, they are ready and safe to cook on. The coals will not often stick to your food. There might be a couple that do—just brush them off when flipping the food. This cooking style can be used for more and more types of meat as you get comfortable with the technique, but I recommend starting with things like skirt steak, oysters, and some of the recipes starting on page 80. It is hot, fast, and quite the showstopper for your friends to watch. You may just want to get the hang of it before getting too experimental, though.

How to build the fire: Building the fire for cooking on coals is, no surprise, like the process for grilling and skillet cooking. You just need to wait for the coals to become white-hot before you use them. If you're eager to make this happen more quickly, use lump charcoal in the charcoal chimney. That is a great alternative for quick coal cooking without waiting for the fire to be ready. Either way, make sure you are ready to cook when the coals are ready. Once you get going, bring your beer because there won't be a break until the food is done.

1. Follow steps 1 through 4 on page 29.

5. Once you have a large amount of blackened and hot wood coals, push them all into one pile. Wait until they are glowing red but white in the middle.

6. Begin to check the fire for your desired cooking temperature.

7. Once the coals are ready, carefully blow off any loose ash on top and begin cooking. As the heat dies, add coals to the outside of the cooking area and push everything into a pile. This will reinvigorate the flames and heat without tampering with the food.

Special equipment: Again, there is not a lot of special equipment needed for cooking on the coals. Use high-quality seasoned wood or lump charcoal and make the choice of which to use intentionally. Waiting for the coals to get white-hot can take a while. Using lump charcoal in a charcoal chimney will speed the process without sacrificing any flavor. If you decide to cook on real wood, be ready to wait 45 minutes to 1 hour to get a solid bed of coals.

INDIRECT FIRE COOKING

The most tender and succulent meat you can find is meat smoked indirectly by a fire. When you use indirect cooking methods, you allow the radiant heat and smoke from the coals to slowly cook your food. This can benefit meat many ways (which I'll dive deeper into later), but the biggest factor is the tenderness that direct cooking cannot achieve. In this book, cooking indirectly does not solely mean "barbecue." I'll also talk about skewers and rotisseries as well as hanging and leaning techniques.

Hanging and leaning are variations of an old technique that works for everything from showstopping meats like Whole Lamb al Asador (page 109), to simple but sublime fruits like Charred and Glazed Pineapple (page 115). Skewers and rotisseries are tools for optimal caramelization of foods without losing crust to sticky surfaces like grill grates. Even classic barbecue smoking can have some twists. In this book, you'll find the secret to faster pork ribs (see Hot and Fast Bourbon-Peach Ribs, page 140) and Salt-Baked Red Snapper (page 146)— but all with the goal of letting smoky aroma surround the food.

Hanging and Leaning

RECIPES START ON PAGE 98.

Description: Using the hanging and leaning cooking styles is an ode to an era without skewers, motorized rotisseries, or enclosed barbecue pits. These are truly classic methods of cooking foods indirectly over a fire and a great place to start an indirect cooking journey. The idea is simple: to place the food next to the fire so the fire's radiant heat slowly cooks it, which makes these techniques suited for larger and more delicate cuts of meat, like whole chicken, a side of salmon, or whole prime rib. By letting the fire gently cook the food, you create great flavor on the outside without losing juiciness inside.

How to build the fire: The fire required for hanging and leaning is not overly complicated, but it does tend to conform to the shape of the food being cooked. The idea is to make a fire that can cook both vertically and horizontally.

There are a couple of ways to tackle this issue, but the main way I accomplish it is by making a "tall" fire. You can do this either by placing the fire next to a fire-resistant wall or by building a stable, taller fire without support. By placing the fire next to a wall, the heat reflects off the wall and bounces back toward the food. This creates that "taller" fire so your food cooks more evenly from top to bottom. If you find yourself without a fire-resistant wall to utilize, place the meat closer to the ground and build the fire both wider and higher than you normally would for direct cooking. This creates the same effect but means the food takes longer to cook.

WALL TECHNIQUE

1. Begin by splitting wood logs into 10 to 12 pieces. Aim for a range of widths, with the most important pieces being the thin shavings.

2. Lay 2 medium-size pieces of wood parallel to each other, about 2 to 3 inches (5 to 7.5 cm) apart. Place natural fire starters in the middle of the 2 logs and light them.

3. Build another layer on top with 2 more similar-size pieces, perpendicular to the logs under them. Between the second layer of logs, add 1 or 2 thin slices of wood that will catch easily.

4. Continue building layers, repeating step 3, until you have 4 to 6 layers. Let the fire burn naturally for 15 to 20 minutes.

5. Once the fire begins to break down, push the fire into a 2- to 2½-foot (60 to 75 cm)-tall pile close to the wall. Start to check the fire for your desired cooking temperature.

6. When ready, begin cooking. Add more wood or lump charcoal, as needed, to maintain the temperature.

NO WALL TECHNIQUE

1. Begin by splitting wood logs into 10 to 12 pieces. Aim for a range of widths, with the most important pieces being the thin shavings.

2. Lay 2 medium-size pieces of wood parallel to each other, about 2 to 3 inches (5 to 7.5 cm) apart. Place natural fire starters in the middle of the 2 logs and light them.

3. Build another layer on top with 2 more similar-size pieces, perpendicular to the logs under them. Between the second layer of logs, add 1 or 2 thin slices of wood that will catch easily.

4. Continue building layers, repeating step 3, until you have 4 to 6 layers. The pile should be 2 to 2½ feet (60 to 75 cm) tall. Repeat this process 2 more times about 1 foot (30 cm) away from the first pile, so you have 3 fires going, 1 foot (30 cm) apart, in a line covering a greater distance and putting out more heat. This will be a 4- to 5-foot (120 to 150 cm)-long fire. Add a couple logs between each fire to connect them. Let this fire break down for 45 minutes to 1 hour.

5. Once the fire begins to break down, place 3 or 4 new logs vertically near the back of the fire (farther away from the food). Continue laying logs until you feel the heat of the fire rise in the air. Begin checking the fire for your desired cooking temperature.

6. When ready, begin cooking. Add more wood or lump charcoal, as needed, to maintain the temperature.

Special equipment: There are a few pieces of really helpful equipment for the hanging and leaning cooking styles. A metal tripod with a metal chain is essential for hanging chicken or prime rib. You should also grab some food-grade stainless-steel nails and wire. Lastly, a stainless-steel Asado cross is the best option for a whole lamb or pig. Sure, most of this can be rigged using equipment you have at home, if needed, but it's best to use food-safe materials and make your life easier— and safer—when cooking with fire.

Skewers/Rotisserie

RECIPES START ON PAGE 119.

Description: I fell in love with this cooking style watching a few Brazilian chefs cooking all kinds of meat over a fire using massive skewers. My first thought was that cooking with, essentially, swords is just cool! But, then, I noticed the meat had the most intense crust because it was barely being touched by the heat from the coals. This blew my mind.

In the United States, skewers tend to be used for direct cooking (and you can make great food that way). However, when I saw that you can cook with them indirectly, I began to see that skewers can elevate food above the coals to get that smoke flavor from a softer, radiant heat. The same thing goes for the rotisserie. From Bacon-Wrapped Maple-Bourbon Chicken Skewers (page 123) to Brazilian-Inspired Picanha (page 126), I encourage you to explore using "metal swords" to cook food in a whole new way.

How to build the fire: To build your fire for cooking with skewers, you'll make a three-zone fire. The zones consist of one side with fire, a middle zone without fire, and another side with fire. The skewer, or rotisserie, is placed between the heat sources so the food cooks slowly with radiant heat, without burning. You can also create this cooking style on a campfire pit or inside a grill using lump charcoal.

1. Begin by splitting wood logs into 10 to 12 pieces. Aim for a range of widths, with the most important pieces being the thin shavings.

2. Lay 2 medium-size pieces of wood parallel to each other, about 2 to 3 inches (5 to 7.5 cm) apart. Place natural fire starters in the middle of the 2 logs and light them.

3. Build another layer on top with 2 more similar-size pieces, perpendicular to the logs under them. Between the second layer of logs, add 1 or 2 thin slices of wood that will catch easily.

4. Continue building layers, repeating step 3, until have 4 to 6 layers. Let the fire burn naturally for 30 to 40 minutes.

5. Once the wood breaks down, push half the wood to one side of the fire and the other half to the opposite side. This creates an empty space between the piles, 1 to 1 ½ feet (30 to 45 cm) apart with the wood about 1 foot (30 cm) high. To prevent flare-ups, place an aluminum foil pan or cast-iron skillet between the fires to catch drippings from the meat. Begin checking the fire for your desired cooking temperature.

6. Once the fire is ready, begin cooking. Watch for flare-ups and add coals or wood, as needed, to maintain the temperature.

Special equipment: The most critical pieces of equipment needed for this style of cooking are skewers and a rotisserie. I prefer long, wide metal skewers (yes, almost like swords). You can grab some online with different variations including two prongs, V shapes, and extra-large skewers. For a rotisserie, I recommend a motorized one. No one wants to sit next to the fire constantly rotating a piece of meat! There are many fantastic rotisseries available that can easily fit over a campfire, your grill, and more.

Barbecue

RECIPES START ON PAGE 136.

Description: For some people, the idea of smoking meat and barbecue, in general, can be intimidating. Cooking whole cuts of meat slowly over fire using nothing but smoke and radiant heat is intoxicating—but also overwhelming. It doesn't help that the flavor from this style of cooking can be extremely delicious—or just plain terrible. On top of that, some cooks can take 10-plus hours of smoking. In this book, my goal is to provide a starter course for dipping your toe into the barbecue pool. I humbly admit there are many other cookbooks to turn to if you want more information on barbecue. But, if you just want a taste of barbecue cooked with live fire, you have come to the right place.

How to build the fire: Building a fire for smoking is easy to do whether you have a legit smoker or a simple setup. The idea is to use a two-zone fire, meaning one side will host the fire itself while the other side remains cooler. This will cook the meat indirectly, so it breaks down slowly. Yes, you are going to need an enclosed grill. Whether you have an offset smoker or a simple kettle, either will work just fine using the same fire style. Feel free to use lump charcoal with wood chunks or chips as your fuel source as well.

1. Begin by splitting wood logs into 10 to 12 pieces. Aim for a range of widths, with the most important pieces being the thin shavings.

2. Lay 2 medium-size pieces of wood parallel to each other, about 2 to 3 inches (5 to 7.5 cm) apart. Place natural fire starters in the middle of the 2 logs and light them.

3. Build another layer on top with 2 more similar-size pieces, perpendicular to the logs under them. Between the second layer of logs, add 1 or 2 thin slices of wood that will catch easily.

4. Continue building layers, repeating step 3, until you have 4 to 6 layers. Let the fire burn naturally for 30 to 40 minutes.

5. Once the wood breaks down into coals, use a shovel to place the hot coals into the hot side of your two-zone fire. You can add these coals to the firebox on your offset smoker as well. For smoke flavor, place a wood log, a couple wood chunks, or a handful of wood chips on top of the coals. Let the white smoke of the wood dissipate before cooking.

6. Keep adding coals and checking the temperature of your smoker until the *cool side* of the grill reaches the desired cooking temperature.

7. Once ready, begin cooking. Continue to add wood to your original fire and let it break down. As coals become ready, keep adding them to the fire to maintain the temperature.

Special equipment: The two essential pieces of equipment for smoking and barbecue are the enclosed smoker and a shovel. There are many excellent grills on the market that can double as smokers. If you get serious about barbecue, I recommend getting a classic offset smoker. For those not interested in that, most enclosed grills will work fine. Either way, make sure you have a sturdy heat-resistant shovel for transferring the hot coals. A bonus piece of equipment would be a burn box, which allows you to keep a roaring fire that will continually create coals for the smoker. If you do not have a burn box, then a fire pit or charcoal chimney will help with replenishing the coals.

2
DIRECT FIRE COOKING

Becoming an expert in fire cooking starts with a firm understanding of the fundamentals. In this chapter, we'll examine the most basic way of cooking: heating meat directly over (or in) the hot coals using limited tools and resources. The tried-and-true direct fire cooking techniques we will explore are grilling, skillet cooking, and cooking on the coals.

Although these three techniques may seem similar, I assure you they conquer the fire in three vastly different ways. Grilling will open doors to get direct char flavor right from the flame. You will unlock delicious smoke from the wood you use to cook, plus you can achieve a nice crust from the intense heat. From seared Skirt Steak with Spicy Cilantro Chimichurri (page 59) to grilled Sweet Adobo Chicken Wings (page 60), this is a great place to start if you want simple but approachable fire grilling.

Cooking with skillets will allow you to cook more delicate foods, for example seafood and eggs. I share my family recipe for Simple Huevos Rancheros (page 65), which is the perfect breakfast dish when you're at a campsite. You will also learn how to baste steaks in cast iron to encapsulate the essence of smoke and butter onto the meat's crust. This is also the place to conquer my famous The Wolf Smashburgers (page 76), which is a beef burger taken to ludicrous extremes.

Last, but certainly not least, is cooking right on the coals. This is not a cheesy party trick, but an epically delicious way of cooking with fire. I'll walk you through searing off steaks on the charcoal's glowing embers, sizzling oysters in the half shell, and roasting an herb-stuffed side of salmon right in the flames. This simple but effective way of cooking with fire results in abundant smoky and caramelized flavors.

GRILLING

Since the discovery of fire, humanity has been learning how to use it as a tool to improve our lives. One of the significant discoveries that came from using fire is grilling. Nowadays, most people use "grilling," as a catch-all term, meaning to cook food over some form of heat using predictable recipes and styles. Although there is nothing wrong with this, I think, sometimes, it is necessary to break from the mold and try new things on the grill.

Since I started my journey with fire, grilling has taken on new meaning. In this chapter, when I refer to "grilling" I mean anything cooked quickly on a grill grate directly above an open flame or hot coals. Often, this means focusing on quick and simple cuts of meat or vegetables—though, in this case, "simple" does not mean lacking in flavor. If you use high-quality ingredients, the food will be some of the most flavorful and enjoyable you've ever eaten.

This style of grilling capitalizes on the preparation before cooking just as much as the char from the flame. Because grilling over direct coals offers only a short period of time to pick up wood-fire flavor, you need to amp up the food before it even touches the grill. One way that we will add extra flavor is by marinating food first—covering meat or veggies in a sauce composed of herbs, spices, citrus, and more—to help tenderize and flavor the food.

Another way we will enhance the food is with a technique called "basting." Basting is a cooking term that refers to melting fat and juices over a piece of meat while it cooks to help retain moisture and enhance flavor. It has other benefits—for example, basting flame-grilled rib eye steaks in a butter sauce adds extra flavor while cooking as the butter drips and creates flares from the fire. In fact, that recipe is where we will begin!

HERB BRUSH–BASTED BONE-IN RIB EYE

There is nothing better than simplicity perfected. This basted rib eye is the first recipe I recommend for those new to cooking over the fire. It is both delicious and easy. Make sure your fire is hot enough for a good sear (see page 22 for checking temperatures). If you are adventurous, make the basting sauce with beef tallow, which is becoming easier to find in more and more grocery stores. Otherwise, use your favorite butter.

PREP TIME: 15 MINUTES | COOK TIME: 20 MINUTES

2 servings

FOR STEAK

2 teaspoons sea salt

2 teaspoons black pepper

2 teaspoons granulated garlic

2 (12-ounce, or 340 g) bone-in rib eye steaks

2 teaspoons olive oil

FOR HERB BRUSH

3 rosemary sprigs

3 thyme sprigs

2 tarragon sprigs

FOR BASTING SAUCE

¼ cup (56 g) unsalted butter or beef tallow

3 garlic cloves, finely chopped

2 teaspoons favorite hot sauce

FOR SPECIAL GEAR

Butcher's twine

Basting saucepan

1. To make the steak: In a small bowl, stir together the salt, pepper, and granulated garlic until thoroughly combined. Lather the rib eyes with oil and dust all sides of the steaks with the seasoning, using it all. Set aside.

2. To make the herb brush: Bundle the herbs sprigs together, wrap some butcher's twine close to the stem ends, and tie it off.

3. Preheat your fire using the instructions for Grilling (see page 29), bringing it to a medium-high temperature (about 375°F, or 190°C).

4. To make the basting sauce: Preheat a saucepan on the grill. Once hot, add all the sauce ingredients. Stir thoroughly, push the pan to the edge of the grill, and keep warm over low heat. Do not boil.

5. Place the steaks on the grill directly over the heat and cook for 2 to 3 minutes per side, flipping and basting the steaks with the herb brush and sauce every minute until the sauce is gone, until they reach your desired internal temperature (I recommend 120°F, or 49°C, for medium-rare). If the steaks are burning or causing flare-ups, pull them to the cooler side of the grill and resume basting until done. If the steaks are not getting enough heat, push your coals closer together and place the steaks on the grill grate above the hot coals.

6. Once done, pull the steaks off the fire and let rest for 7 to 8 minutes before slicing and serving, or serve the steaks whole.

How to Make an Herb Brush for Basting

For me, the cornerstone to a grilled steak is basting it. You get that insane outside crust and flavor, especially when you use an herb brush to apply the baste. It is simple to make an herb brush at home. Bonus: When you are done basting, add the herb brush to your coals for a nice herbal essence to your steak right at the end!

1. Grab some fresh herbs—I prefer 2 sprigs each of rosemary, thyme, and tarragon—and 10 to 12 inches (25 to 30 cm) of butcher's twine.
2. Lay the herbs flat in a bundle and cross the string over the stem ends.
3. Securely tie the herbs with the string. Cut off any excess string.
4. Dip the herbs into your basting sauce and baste away.

SPATCHCOCK BRICK-PRESSED LEMON-CHILI CHICKEN

This chicken is an ode to my grilling experiences living in the South. Pro tip: Wrap your brick in aluminum foil and preheat it before cooking. Spatchcocking the chicken (see sidebar, page 55) helps the chicken cook faster. The brick also speeds the process, and when preheated, acts as a cooking surface as well. The lemon-chili sauce resembles a peri peri sauce in flavor.

PREP TIME: 30 MINUTES | MARINATING TIME: 4 HOURS OR OVERNIGHT | COOK TIME: 45 MINUTES

4 servings

1 (3- to 4-pound, or 1.36 to 1.8 kg) whole chicken

1 recipe Lemon-Chili Marinade (page 190)

FOR SPECIAL GEAR

2 clean bricks wrapped in aluminum foil

Basting brush

1. Place the whole chicken on a work surface, breast-side down. Using a sharp knife, remove the backbone by cutting alongside it on both sides, being careful to cut as little as possible into the meat or the oyster. (The oyster of the chicken is a delicacy. The two oysters are found on the back of the chicken near the thigh in a hollow part of the bone.) Remove the backbone (save it for making chicken stock).

2. Flip the chicken and firmly press on the breastbone until it cracks and allows the bird to lay flat. Trim any excess fat or skin. Place the chicken into a food-safe container for marinating.

3. Measure and set aside 2 tablespoons of marinade for basting. Cover and refrigerate.

4. Lather the remaining marinade all over the chicken. Cover and refrigerate to marinate for at least 4 hours or, ideally, overnight.

5. Preheat your fire using the instructions for Grilling (see page 29), waiting until the coals become white-hot throughout, or the temperature registers medium, 300°F (150°C) before moving on.

6. Place the foil-wrapped bricks on the grill to preheat for 5 minutes.

7. Pull the chicken out of the marinade and discard the marinade. Place the chicken on the grill directly over the heat, skin-side down. Place the bricks on top of the chicken and cook for 10 minutes, or until the chicken begins to hold an amber-brown color on the outside edges.

recipe continues

8. Remove the bricks and flip the chicken, bone-side down, placing it on a cooler part of the grill. Baste the chicken with the reserved marinade and cook for 15 to 20 minutes, or until the internal temperature reaches 165°F (74°C) and the chicken is orange-ish-red in color. If the chicken begins to have flare-ups, pull it to a cooler side of the grill and continue to cook. Pull the chicken off the grill and let rest for 5 minutes before slicing. I prefer to cut mine into 8 sections to serve.

How to Spatchcock Chicken

Whole chicken can be a long cook over a fire. Luckily, there is an easy way to speed up the process—called spatchcocking. You remove the chicken's backbone, so it lays flat, cooks more quickly and evenly, and develops a nice, crispy skin. Try it! You'll need a whole chicken and a sharp knife or kitchen shears:

1. Place the chicken on a cutting board, breast-side down.
2. Guide your knife along the spine on both sides from the neck to the tail, removing only the spine.
3. Turn the chicken breast-side up and firmly press on the breastbone to break it, so the chicken lays flat.
4. Get your fire ready to cook!

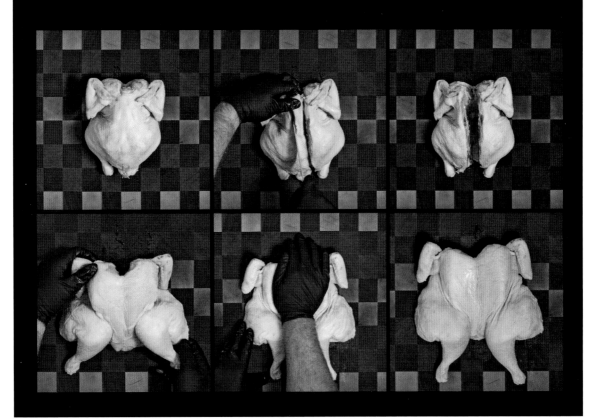

HONEY ESPRESSO–GLAZED PORK CHOPS

For the coffee lovers, this a great recipe for direct grilling. For my noncoffee lovers, you're wrong . . . just kidding! But you might want to skip this one, or switch out the marinade. As written, this recipe will kick you into high gear. It is a savory-sweet blend with a punch and a nice nutty finish. If you do not have espresso, use strongly brewed drip coffee.

PREP TIME: 2 HOURS 20 MINUTES | COOK TIME: 15 MINUTES

4 servings

FOR HONEY ESPRESSO GLAZE

½ cup (120 ml) espresso or strongly brewed coffee

2 tablespoons (30 ml) balsamic vinegar

1 tablespoon (10 g) chopped shallot

1 tablespoon (20 g) honey

2 teaspoons sea salt

2 teaspoons black pepper

1 teaspoon fresh thyme leaves

FOR PORK CHOPS

4 (10-ounce, or 280 g) pork chops (preferably bone-in)

2 teaspoons olive oil

1 tablespoon (18 g) sea salt

1 tablespoon (6 g) black pepper

1 tablespoon (8.4 g) smoked paprika

1 teaspoon onion powder

FOR SPECIAL GEAR

Basting saucepan

Basting brush

1. To make the honey espresso glaze: In a blender, combine all the glaze ingredients. Blend until smooth. Transfer to a bowl, cover, and refrigerate for at least 2 hours to let the flavors meld.

2. To make the pork chops: Lather the chops with oil and season both sides with salt, pepper, paprika, and onion powder. Set aside.

3. Preheat your fire using the instructions for Grilling (see page 29), bringing it to a medium-high temperature (about 350°F, or 180°C).

4. Place the pork chops on the grill directly over the heat and cook for 5 to 6 minutes until the pork begins to take on an amber-golden color on the outside edges. Flip the pork chops and cook for 5 to 6 minutes more.

5. Preheat a saucepan on the cool side of the fire, to prevent the glaze from burning. Add the glaze to the saucepan and let it heat for 1 minute.

6. When the pork chops are close to being done, use a basting brush to glaze the chops. Flip them once or twice to glaze thoroughly, then let sit over the heat to caramelize.

7. When the chops reach an internal temperature of 145°F (63°C), pull them off the fire and let rest for 5 minutes. Top with a little more glaze before slicing and enjoying.

SKIRT STEAK WITH SPICY CILANTRO CHIMICHURRI

This skirt steak is a riff on the first recipe I ever made when I started my journey with *Over The Fire Cooking*. As you might expect for such a special recipe, I have cooked it many times since and have slowly perfected it. Remember, skirt steak is a thin cut of meat so it will cook faster than a normal (thicker) cut of beef. As for the chimichurri, it may not be traditional (see page 179 for my take on Classic Chimichurri), but this spicy sauce is out of this world in flavor.

PREP TIME: 20 MINUTES | COOK TIME: 20 MINUTES

4 servings

1 or 2 outside skirt steaks, silverskin removed

2 teaspoons olive oil

1 tablespoon (18 g) sea salt

1 tablespoon (6 g) black pepper

2 teaspoons chipotle powder

1 recipe Spicy Cilantro Chimichurri (page 180)

1. Lather the skirt steaks with oil and season all over with salt, pepper, and chipotle powder. Refrigerate for 15 minutes.

2. Preheat your fire using the instructions for Grilling (see page 29), bringing it to a high temperature (about 400°F, or 200°C).

3. Place the steaks over the fire and cook for about 2 minutes per side, or until they reach your desired internal temperature (I recommend 120°F, or 49°C, for medium-rare). Pull the steaks off the fire and let rest for 7 to 8 minutes.

4. While your steaks rest, pull the chimichurri sauce from the refrigerator and let it come to room temperature.

5. Slice your skirt steak by first cutting with the grain into 3- to 4-inch (7.5 to 10 cm) segments. Rotate the segments 90 degrees and cut them against the grain into ¼-inch 0.6 cm) slices. Top the steak with the spicy cilantro chimichurri and serve.

SWEET ADOBO CHICKEN WINGS

Although I might strike you as a steak-kinda guy, I absolutely love grilled chicken wings. These wings, in particular, are the perfect flavor blend for those who need some spice, tang, and sweetness all in one bite. You should easily find all the ingredients at your local grocery; if you have trouble finding chipotles in adobo sauce, substitute 1 fresh jalapeño. Roast it over the fire for 2 to 3 minutes 'til the outsides are charred. Chop them, add to the blender, and you are ready to go.

PREP TIME: 15 MINUTES | MARINATING TIME: 4 HOURS | COOK TIME: 20 MINUTES

4 servings

½ (7-ounce, or 200 g) can chipotle peppers in adobo sauce

6 tablespoons (6 g) chopped fresh cilantro, divided

2 tablespoons (20 g) chopped red onion

1 serrano pepper, stemmed

1½ tablespoons (27 g) kosher salt

Juice of 2 limes

Grated zest of 2 limes

2 pounds (908 g) chicken wings, flats and drums separated

3 tablespoons (60 g) agave nectar

1. In a blender, combine the chipotles in adobo, 4 tablespoons (4 g) of cilantro, the red onion, serrano, salt, lime juice, and lime zest. Blend just until smooth.

2. Place the chicken wings into a large bowl and add the marinade. Toss to coat. Cover the bowl and refrigerate for at least 4 hours or, ideally, overnight, letting the marinade work.

3. Preheat your fire using the instructions for Grilling (see page 29). Wait until the coals become white-hot throughout or until the fire temperature reaches medium, 300°F (150°C), before moving on.

4. Remove the chicken wings from the refrigerator and drain the excess marinade. Discard the marinade. Transfer the wings to the grill. Cook for 8 to 10 minutes total, flipping the wings every 2 minutes to cook evenly. Using a temperature probe, once the chicken's internal temperature reaches 165°F (74°C) and the wings have a nice char, use tongs to transfer the wings to a heat-safe bowl and top them with the agave. Toss until evenly coated. Plate the wings and garnish with the remaining 2 tablespoons (2 g) of cilantro.

SKILLET

Talk to any fire cook and they will tell you they never leave the house without their cast-iron skillet. For me, the skillet is so essential I treat it like an extension of my body. The reason it is so sacred is that it can be used so many ways—from searing off delicate pieces of seafood to getting the perfect crust on a smashburger. The skillet opens new doors for those who want to master open-fire cooking.

Food for thought: Have you ever tried to cook an egg on the grill without a skillet? I'll tell you how it ends . . . you get coal-roasted scrambled eggs. While cooking on coals is an awesome technique (just wait 'til page 80), I prefer my eggs not covered in crunchy ash. Again, the skillet comes to the rescue, giving you the option to cook in a contained space.

A lot of people have asked me if you can get wood-fire flavor in a cast-iron skillet. The short answer is, yes. You get wood-fire flavor anytime you cook food in the presence of smoke or burning logs. While it may not be as intense as grilling a steak directly over coals, a lot of food ideal for cooking in cast iron does not need a ton of smoke flavor anyway.

In this section I revisit the world of basting using a simple butter basting sauce for rib eye (see page 68) and Honey Espresso–Glazed Pork Chops (page 56). For seafood lovers, I teach you how to sear off some Sweet and Spicy Glazed Scallops (page 72) along with some quickly marinated Chili-Lime Shrimp (page 75) with a zesty flair. I also share two family favorites: The Wolf Smashburgers (page 76) and Simple Huevos Rancheros (page 65). These are longtime favorites at my house that I am finally writing down the recipes for everyone to enjoy! Now, let's jump right into some breakfast with those huevos.

SIMPLE HUEVOS RANCHEROS

One of the first meals I ate around the fire was huevos rancheros. My father, having spent a lot of time in Mexico for work, fell in love with this dish. My take on this favorite meal shows how easy and delicious it can be. Don't have time to make the Charred Salsa Verde? Do not worry—almost any salsa can work with this dish. For a little extra flavor, roast the tortillas on the coals or grill grate for 30 seconds.

PREP TIME: 20 MINUTES | COOK TIME: 15 MINUTES

2 servings

2 tablespoons (30 ml) olive oil

4 large eggs

4 (6-inch, or 15 cm) corn tortillas

1 (15-ounce, or 425 g) can black beans, drained and rinsed

1 recipe Charred Salsa Verde (page 182)

¼ cup shredded Cotija cheese

1 teaspoon chopped fresh cilantro

FOR SPECIAL GEAR

Cast-iron skillet

Wooden spoon

1. Preheat your fire using the instructions for the Skillet method (see page 30), bringing it to a medium-high temperature (about 375°F, or 190°C). Pour the oil into a cast-iron skillet and place it over the coals for 2 minutes to preheat before cooking.

2. One at a time, crack the eggs into a small bowl to avoid any eggshell getting into the skillet and add the egg to the skillet. Cook to your preference. I like mine sunny-side up, so I cook it for 2 minutes until the yolk is no longer liquidy. Pull the eggs out of the skillet and set aside.

3. Discard any excess oil in the skillet and return it to the fire. Warm the tortillas in the skillet for 30 seconds per side until slightly toasted. Finally, add the black beans to the skillet and stir while cooking for 1 minute until they are fully warmed.

4. To make your huevos, start with a warm tortilla. Top the tortilla with a scoop of black beans, then add 1 egg. Cover the egg in salsa, garnish with some Cotija cheese, and add a pinch of cilantro. Repeat.

Cleaning and Caring for Cast Iron

Cooking with cast iron takes a little love and care to make it last and deliver its best results. Little things can go a long way to help keep your cast-iron skillets primed and ready for fire cooking!

x **Seasoning your skillet:** Whether a brand-new skillet or an heirloom piece, your skillet needs to be seasoned. There are a few ways to do this—the most obvious is to cook in it a lot. Cooking in your skillet, then cleaning it properly, retains the seasoning and keeps it ready to use. Otherwise, try this:

1. Wash your skillet under hot running water and scrub it with a brush.
2. Coat the skillet in a thin layer of oil (preferably vegetable oil or shortening).
3. Preheat the oven to 375°F (190°C).
4. Place your skillet in the oven, face-down, with an aluminum foil pan underneath to catch the drippings, and bake for 1 hour.
5. With oven mitts, remove the skillet, wipe off the excess oil, and let cool. Repeat this process 2 or 3 times until the skillet is smooth and well-seasoned.

x **Cleaning your skillet:** All you need to clean your skillet are hot water, a sturdy brush, and elbow grease. Please do not use soap on cast iron as it will remove the layer of seasoning you have built on it! Rinse the skillet under hot water and scrub out the dirty parts. If this gives you some trouble, simmer a small amount of red wine in the skillet over high heat for 2 to 3 minutes to releases the stuck-on bits. Don't reduce the wine too much or it will become part of the problem. Dry the skillet completely, then add 1 tablespoon (15 ml) of oil to the skillet and wipe it down with a paper towel. I do this after every cook to keep the seasoning intact.

x **Storing your skillet:** When your skillet is properly cleaned and completely dry, I recommend storing it in the cupboard away from water and moisture to keep it from rusting. If it does rust a little, lather some oil over it and it should be good to go. If it goes too far, start the seasoning process from the beginning.

SALT-PEPPER-CINNAMON RIB EYE WITH BUTTER BASTE

Remember the Herb Brush–Basted Bone-In Rib Eye (page 49)? We basted it with an herb brush. Here, I show you how to baste the steak in its own juices inside a cast-iron skillet. A few tips for those who want to knock this out of the park: 1. Lower the temperature of your fire and skillet before you baste. Butter has a bad tendency to burn over high heat. 2. Okay, yes, lowering the temperature is not as easy with a fire as when using the stove. Lowering a fire's temperature can be done quickly, though, by spreading out the coals or removing some coals from the fire. Don't overthink it! 3. Place the garlic on the steak *while basting* as it will melt into the steak while cooking.

PREP TIME: 15 MINUTES | COOK TIME: 15 MINUTES

1 serving

2 teaspoons sea salt

2 teaspoons black pepper

1 teaspoon ground cinnamon

1 bone-in rib eye

Canola oil

¼ cup (56 g) unsalted butter

3 or 4 garlic cloves, unpeeled

FOR SPECIAL GEAR:

Cast-iron skillet

Basting spoon

1. In a small bowl, thoroughly mix the salt, pepper, and cinnamon.

2. Lather the steak with oil. Season all sides of the steak with the spices, making sure not to miss the sides. Set the steaks on a plate, cover, and refrigerate for 10 minutes.

3. Preheat your fire using the instructions for the Skillet method (see page 30), bringing it to a medium-high temperature (about 375°F, or 190°C).

4. Preheat a cast-iron skillet over the fire with a touch of oil in it for 2 minutes before cooking.

5. Add the rib eye to the skillet and sear each side for 30 to 45 seconds. Shoot for a nice crust everywhere, so sear the edges of the steak on the sides of the skillet, if necessary.

6. Pull the skillet off the fire and lower the temperature of the fire to a medium heat (about 325°F, or 170°C).

7. Add the butter to the skillet to melt. Place the steak into the skillet and place the garlic on top of the steak. Cook for about 2 minutes, basting the warm butter over the steak with a spoon. Flip the steak, arrange the garlic back on top, and continue cooking and basting for 2 to 3 minutes, or until it reaches an internal temperature of 120°F (49°C) for medium-rare, or to your desired doneness. Pull the steak off the fire, cover, and let rest for 7 to 8 minutes. Serve the steak whole with a side of vegetables, if you like.

Three Simple Steak Seasonings

When it comes to seasoning steak, there are so many flavors that can make your taste buds explode. Although some people like to keep things simple, with just salt and pepper, here are three unique steak seasonings that will make a flavor impression without being overpowering. Each makes enough for two New York strips or two rib eyes:

1. **SPG**: This seasoning comprises only three ingredients—salt, pepper, and garlic— but it really makes steak delicious. SPG is the holy trinity of steak seasonings as it complements just about anything! Add to rib eye, sirloin, or even burger patties for authentic meat flavor.

   Ingredients: Equal parts kosher salt, freshly cracked black pepper, and granulated garlic

2. **Savory Coffee Rub**: Coffee makes an excellent (and somewhat surprising) seasoning for steaks. It creates a delicious caramelized crust with an essence of cocoa. Pair finely ground coffee with brown sugar (or granulated sugar), and you have a winning combo. Add this to a fatty bone-in rib eye, whole prime rib, or filet mignon for a nice savory yet sweet bite.

   Ingredients: 1 tablespoon (18 g) kosher salt, 2 teaspoons finely ground coffee, 2 teaspoons black pepper, 2 teaspoons light brown sugar, 2 teaspoons garlic powder, and 2 teaspoons onion powder

3. **Simple Cajun Rub**: If you are a fan of spicy seasoning, this rub is for you. This simple Cajun seasoning is basic but packs lots of heat. Season skirt steak, flank steak, or flap steak with this and you will pat yourself on the back for a job well done. Add some oil to make a paste, as the seasoning can char when cooked over high temperatures.

   Ingredients: 2 teaspoons garlic powder, 2 teaspoons smoked paprika, 1½ teaspoons kosher salt, 1½ teaspoons black pepper, 1 teaspoon dried oregano, 1 teaspoon onion powder, ½ teaspoon cayenne pepper, and ½ teaspoon red pepper flakes

SWEET AND SPICY GLAZED SCALLOPS

Scallops are one of my favorite things to cook over the fire. As with other delicate foods, you need a skillet to get the right texture on the scallops. Although they are not as sturdy as steak, you do not need to be super gentle with them either. They cook best if you work quickly over really high heat. The key for getting a good crust on scallops, in addition to the high heat, is making sure they are super dry. Pat them dry with a paper towel and, if you have the time, let them rest in the fridge to cool and continue to dry. When you combine them with a hot skillet, you're primed for great results!

PREP TIME: 15 MINUTES, PLUS 3 HOURS TO REFRIGERATE (OPTIONAL) | COOK TIME: 10 MINUTES

2 servings

FOR SCALLOPS

10 to 12 bay scallops, patted dry with paper towel

Oil

2 teaspoons sea salt

Sesame seeds, for garnish

Finely sliced scallions, for garnish

FOR SWEET AND SPICY GLAZE

1 tablespoon (15 ml) soy sauce

1 tablespoon (20 g) honey

1½ teaspoons chili paste

Juice of 1 lime

Juice of 1 orange

FOR SPECIAL GEAR

Cast-iron skillet

1. To make the scallops: If you have time, refrigerate the patted-dry scallops for 2 to 3 hours to continue to dry.

2. To make the sweet and spicy glaze: In a small food-safe bowl, stir together all the glaze ingredients. Set aside.

3. To finish the scallops: Preheat your fire using the instructions for the Skillet method (see page 30), bringing it to a high temperature (about 450°F, or 230°C).

4. Preheat a cast-iron skillet with a small touch of oil in it over the fire for 2 minutes before cooking.

5. Season the scallops all over with salt and add them to the hot skillet. If you hear an immediate sizzle, you have the right temperature; if not, increase the temperature and keep cooking. Cook for about 1 minute, then flip the scallops—placing them on a spot in the skillet that has not been used previously to get a good crust on both sides. Cook for 1 to 1½ minutes until the scallops are no longer translucent but opaque. Pull the skillet off the fire and let rest for 1 to 2 minutes.

6. Lightly brush the scallops with the remaining glaze while still in the skillet, then garnish with sesame seeds and scallions to serve.

CHILI-LIME SHRIMP

Citrusy, spicy shrimp are a crave-worthy food, and this recipe is what I like to make when that inevitable craving strikes. Shrimp cook very fast compared to other proteins that I recommend for the skillet. If you are having trouble telling when your shrimp are done, look at their shape. Perfectly cooked shrimp form a "C"—the ends should not touch, but be barely curved so they make the letter C. If all your shrimp look like an "O," they're likely overcooked to the point of rubbery. Time to try again.

PREP TIME: 15 MINUTES | MARINATING TIME: 1 HOUR | COOK TIME: 10 MINUTES

2 servings

FOR CHILI-LIME MARINADE

1 tablespoon (22 g) achiote paste

2 tablespoons (34 g) chipotle peppers in adobo sauce

2 tablespoons (2 g) chopped fresh cilantro

2 teaspoons sea salt

Juice of 2 limes

Juice of 1 orange

FOR SHRIMP

2 pounds (90 g) shrimp, peeled and deveined

Oil

Chopped fresh cilantro, for garnish

Lime wedges, for garnish

FOR SPECIAL GEAR

Cast-iron skillet

1. To make the chili-lime marinade: In a large bowl, thoroughly whisk all the marinade ingredients to combine.

2. To make the shrimp: Add the shrimp to the marinade and gently toss to coat evenly. Refrigerate the shrimp to marinate for 1 hour, but no more than 2 hours.

3. Preheat your fire using the instructions for the Skillet method (see page 30), bringing it to a medium-high temperature (about 375°F, or 190°C).

4. Preheat a cast-iron skillet with a touch of oil in it over the fire for 1 to 2 minutes before cooking.

5. Once the skillet is hot but not smoking, remove the shrimp from the marinade and place them in the skillet. Discard the marinade. Cook the shrimp for 4 to 5 minutes until they turn from translucent to whitish-orange in color, stirring occasionally. Pull the shrimp off the fire and let rest for 1 minute. Serve with a touch of cilantro on top, lime wedges for squeezing, and a side of rice and beans, if you like.

THE WOLF SMASHBURGER

The idea for The Wolf Smashburger started, not at home, but in Ireland. At a live cooking event, a fellow chef wanted me to build my own burger. He was cooking all kinds of dishes that day, including a smoked picanha. I love picanha (see page 126), so I built this burger as an ode to everything I love about South American food—with a little American fusion. Don't have picanha? Use rib eye, sirloin, or tri-tip.

PREP TIME: 30 MINUTES | COOK TIME: 1 HOUR

4 servings

FOR BURGERS AND STEAK

3 tablespoons (54 g) sea salt

3 tablespoons (18 g) black pepper

3 tablespoons (27 g) garlic powder

1 whole (2- to 3-pound, or 908 g to 1.36 kg) picanha/ top sirloin cap

1½ tablespoons (23 ml) olive oil, plus more as needed

1 pound (454 g) 80/20 ground chuck

8 bacon slices

4 slices American cheese

FOR SERVING THE BURGERS

4 brioche burger buns

2 tablespoons (28 g) unsalted butter, at room temperature

4 tablespoons (60 g) mayonnaise

1 recipe Classic Chimichurri (page 179)

FOR SPECIAL GEAR

2 large cast-iron skillets

Spatula

Burger press (optional)

1. To make the burgers and steak: In a small bowl, stir together the salt, pepper, and garlic powder.

2. Lather the outside of the picanha with oil and season the steak thoroughly with one-third of the spices.

3. Roll the ground chuck into 4 (4-ounce, or 115 g) balls. Lather the burger balls in oil and season all over with another one-third of the spice mix. Refrigerate until you are ready to cook.

4. Preheat your fire using the instructions for the Skillet method (see page 30), bringing it to a medium-high temperature (about 375°F, or 190°C).

5. Either add the picanha to a cast-iron skillet and place it over the fire, or place the meat directly onto the grill grate over the fire, fat-side down. Sear all sides of the steak for about 1 minute per side and 2 minutes on the fat-cap. Pull the steak off the fire.

6. Cut the picanha from side to side (not top to tail) into steaks about 1½ inches (3.5 cm) thick. Lather the steaks again with oil and season any unseasoned parts with the remaining spice mix. Return the steaks to the grill and cook for 2 to 4 minutes per side until they reach an internal temperature of 120°F (49°C) for medium-rare, or to your desired doneness. The fat cap on the outside of the steak should stay about ½ inch (1 cm) thick, but you can render it down further, if you like. Once the steaks are done, pull them off the fire, cover, and set aside to rest while you cook the bacon and burgers.

7. Preheat a large cast-iron skillet over the fire for 2 minutes before cooking.

recipe continues

8. In the skillet, arrange the bacon slices. Cook for 3 to 4 minutes, or until cooked to your preference. Pull the bacon off the fire, cover to keep warm, and set aside. Drain the grease from the skillet and return it to the fire.

9. Add the burger balls to the skillet. Cook for 30 seconds. Cover the balls with parchment paper. One at a time, to get a good crust, press down firmly on the balls using a spatula or burger press. Hold the press for 30 seconds. Cook the patties for 2 minutes. Flip the patties, top each with 1 slice of cheese, and cook for 2 minutes more. If possible, cover the skillet so the cheese melts evenly. Once the burgers are crispy and browned throughout, pull them off the fire and set aside.

10. To serve the burgers: Lather the cut side of the burger buns with butter and place over the fire for 30 seconds to crisp the insides.

11. Now it is time to build your burger! Thinly slice the picanha steaks. Place a dollop of mayonnaise on a burger bun bottom. Add 1 smashburger patty, 2 bacon slices, a second smashburger patty, 3 or 4 slices of picanha, a spoonful of chimichurri, and the burger bun top. Repeat.

12. Serve the burgers with a side of fries or onion rings—if you think you'll have room.

History of The Wolf Burger

During the summer of 2018, I was invited to Dublin, Ireland, to participate in a cooking festival called The Big Grill. It's one of the largest outdoor cooking festivals in the world, so I was excited and honored they wanted me there. While travelling to the event, I was eager to connect with so many talented fire cooks from around the world—all in one place.

The event did not disappoint. It was one of the best and most inspirational experiences of my life. There were so many techniques to learn—from buried goat to hanging trout—and all from world-class experts in experimental fire cooking. I was like a fly on the wall, taking in everything.

While there, I befriended an Irish chef named John Relihan. He had a massive fire-cooking burger stand with a line of fans stretching out the door. We became fast friends while I photographed the crazy burger creations he was cooking and selling. In the middle of all the hustle and bustle, he asked me if I would like to create a special burger. Of course!—so, together, we dove into making something that would represent Over The Fire Cooking.

We started with two large burger patties, bacon, and cheese. Next, came slices of the picanha he was grilling, with chimichurri topping it all—and the original Wolf Burger was born! It was an instant hit, with John selling them right in the middle of the festival. A couple months later, at his burger restaurant in downtown Dublin, John featured The Wolf Burger. It sold out—and continues to sell out every time he brings it back to the menu. Reflecting on my experience, that festival remains a highlight of my cooking career.

Since then, I have worked to perfect the recipe John and I created. I've switched up the patties and landed on smashburgers because I like the texture and it keeps the burger's height within reason. With a few edits to my own Classic Chimichurri (page 179), we now have The Wolf Burger 2.0. Just remember, when making your own Wolf Smashburgers (page 76), a lot of love, fun, and beer went into this burger's creation.

COOKING ON THE COALS

Are you curious about unique ways of cooking with fire? (If you are like me, you probably skipped everything to get right here.) Let's talk about cooking on the coals!

What is it about fire that gets us so fired up? It awakens something inside our inner being that is drawn to its warmth while in awe of its wild unpredictability. For those who dare to step beyond the more popular cooking methods and attempt to cook on the coals, there is a prize waiting for you: delicious ember-roasted food.

One of the first questions I get before teaching about cooking on the coals is whether food will taste like ash. In short, no. That said, you might have a little ash from the coals on your food. Usually, all you need to do to avoid unnecessary ash is to start your fire correctly and use the right equipment. Refer to the section on how to build your fire for cooking on the coals (see page 33) to make sure you are set up for success.

Now, let's talk about the food. In this section, I cover my favorite style of coal roasting. The basic idea I embrace is to use less fatty, more quick-cooking foods and throw them right on the embers until they are fully done.

We will start with a favorite: Coal-Roasted Lobster Tails (page 83) topped with a lemon-garlic butter sauce. Next, we tackle Dirty Chipotle New York Strips. Although this might seem scandalous, I promise it is absolutely delicious. Then, we try Campfire Hot Salmon (page 88) and Herb Butter Oysters on the Half Shell (page 91)—yes, you can cook oysters on the coals! Finally, we throw a curveball with the Spicy Lamb Chops (page 94). I have to say, this is one of my favorite ways to cook, so let's get those coals started!

COAL-ROASTED LOBSTER TAILS

When you're cooking on the coals, it doesn't get any better than proteins like lobster tails, which have a thick outer layer to protect them from the fire and ash. After falling in love with this from chef Steven Raichlen, my biggest tip for this cook is to make sure you slice them right. Double check that you do not break too much of the shell when cutting them in half. Additionally, keep glazing them with butter sauce while cooking, as the butter melts into the meat—if you do it right, it's almost as if the lobsters are being poached.

PREP TIME: 30 MINUTES | COOK TIME: 10 MINUTES

4 servings

FOR LOBSTER TAILS

4 fresh lobster tails

Olive oil

2 teaspoons sea salt

2 teaspoons black pepper

1 teaspoon garlic powder

1 teaspoon ground cumin

Chopped fresh parsley, for garnish

Lemon wedges, for garnish

FOR LEMON-GARLIC BUTTER

¼ cup (56 g) unsalted butter

4 garlic cloves, minced

Juice of 1 lemon

2 tablespoons (8 g) finely chopped fresh parsley

FOR SPECIAL GEAR

Saucepan

Spoon

1. To make the lobster tails: Place the lobster tails on a work surface. Place your knife at the top of the tail and slice lengthwise down the spine, splitting it all the way through. Try your best to leave part of the top and the tail slightly connected so you end up with one lobster tail split in half. Fold open the tail, so the meat shows and the shell is on the back. Lather the lobster tails with oil and season thoroughly with salt, pepper, garlic powder, and cumin.

2. Preheat your fire using the instructions for Cooking on the Coals (see page 33). Once your coals are white-hot, blow off any ash on top. The fire temperature should be medium-high (about 375°F, or 190°C).

3. To make the lemon-garlic butter: Preheat a saucepan over the fire for 1 minute. In the pan, combine the lemon-garlic butter sauce ingredients and let them melt to combine.

4. To finish the lobster tails: Place the lobster tails, meat-side down, directly on the coals. Cook for 2 minutes. Look for the edges of the shell to turn from orange to red. Once they are reddish all around, flip the tails, brush off any coal or excess ash, and cook for 2 to 3 minutes, or until they are no longer translucent and reach an internal temperature of about 135°F (57°C).

5. After the flip, cover the lobster tails in the butter sauce. Keep basting them in the butter sauce until they are done. Pull the lobster tails off the fire and let cool for 2 minutes.

6. Serve the lobster tails, meat-side up, garnished with parsley, with lemon wedges for squeezing, and a glaze of leftover sauce.

DIRTY CHIPOTLE NEW YORK STRIPS

When I got into coal-roasting food, one of the first things I cooked was a New York strip. Unlike lobster and shellfish, there is obviously no protective layer on steak! However, this cut of steak is ideal for this cooking style because it is full of flavor throughout—but without a ton of thick fat that will burn on the coals. Cook these steaks for only a few minutes per side until they are nice and toasty. For those worried about ash, don't be! The crust develops so fast with the steak on the hot coals that the ash will not stick. I like to top this steak with a little butter while it rests for extra flavor.

PREP TIME: 30 MINUTES | COOK TIME: 10 MINUTES

4 servings

4 New York strip steaks

Olive oil

1 recipe Chipotle Rub (page 191)

4 tablespoons (56 g) unsalted butter

Chopped fresh cilantro, for garnish

1. Lather the steaks with oil. Season the steaks thoroughly with the chipotle rub and refrigerate to rest for 15 minutes.

2. Preheat your fire using the instructions for Cooking on the Coals (see page 33). Once your coals are white-hot, blow off any excess ash on top. The fire temperature should be medium-high (about 375°F, or 190°C).

3. Carefully place your steaks directly on the coals. Cook for about 3 minutes. As the sides of the steak begin to caramelize and char, carefully lift the steaks, dust off any coals that cling to the meat, flip it over, and place the steaks back on the coals. Cook this side for about 3 minutes until they reach an internal temperature of 120°F (49°C), or to your preferred doneness. Add a little chipotle rub to any spot where the seasoning has fallen off, if desired.

4. Pull the steaks off the fire and top each with 1 tablespoon (14 g) of butter. Cover the steaks and let rest for 7 to 8 minutes. To serve the steak, slice it and top with a little cilantro.

Tips for Cooking on the Coals

There are few rules when it comes to fire cooking, in general. That said, cooking on the coals might be a new world for many, so a few tips and tricks can go a long way.

Use real wood or lump charcoal: We all care about where our food comes from and knowing it is the highest quality. The same should go for the wood you use to cook the food. Using real wood or natural lump charcoal as your only fuel source when cooking on the coals is important because briquettes and other compressed charcoal carry chemicals that are ideal for grilling but not for placing your food right on top of.

Avoid cooking in high-airflow grills: Cooking on the coals is intended for meals that take a short amount of time to cook. The food tends to caramelize quickly and can even get slightly burnt on the outer edges. With grills that use high airflows, like kettles, kamado-style, or even some fire pits, the airflow is perfect for long cooking periods but can make the coals too hot. Try cooking in a simple fire pit or somewhere with low airflow underneath the coals, which allows you to cook your food without burning it.

Use good equipment: We talked about equipment in Getting Started (see page 13), but what about gear needed for cooking on coals? Luckily, that list is not that different. I carry with me a solid pair of fire-resistant gloves, a pitchfork, and tongs. The fire-resistant gloves help keep your hands from burning. The pitchfork is ideal for breaking down the wood into coals or for pushing it around into nice piles and the tongs are ideal for flipping those steaks or repositioning your coal-roasted flatbread (see page 163).

CAMPFIRE HOT SALMON

Salmon cooked directly on the coals . . . am I crazy? No. To cook this salmon, we are not going to put it directly on the coals like the Dirty Chipotle New York Strips (page 84). Instead, we will bake the salmon inside aluminum foil, which will be covered in hot coals. Once you get the hang of it, try this method with other fish, like sea bass, rainbow trout, or arctic char. You can also vary the seasonings, but I encourage you to try the recipe as-is first: the tenderness of the fish along with spicy heat and honey flavor are all you need.

PREP TIME: 45 MINUTES | COOK TIME: 10 MINUTES

4 servings

FOR SEASONING

1 tablespoon (12.5 g) cane sugar

1 tablespoon (18 g) kosher salt

1½ teaspoons onion powder

1 teaspoon chili powder

1 teaspoon sweet paprika

1 teaspoon garlic powder

1 teaspoon cayenne pepper

1 teaspoon black pepper

½ teaspoon smoked paprika

FOR SALMON

10 to 12 kale or lettuce leaves

1 whole side of salmon, ideally king salmon

Canola oil

5 or 6 lemons, cut into slices

FOR HONEY BUTTER

½ cup (112 g) unsalted butter

2 tablespoons (40 g) honey

FOR SPECIAL GEAR

Cast-iron skillet

1. To make the seasoning: In a small bowl, stir together all the seasoning ingredients.

2. Preheat your fire using the instructions for Cooking on the Coals (see page 33), bringing it to a medium temperature (about 325°F, or 170°C).

3. To make the salmon: Cut 2 aluminum foil pieces 1½ times the size of your salmon. Lay the strips on top of each other, creating a double layer. Place a piece of parchment paper about the same size as the foil on top.

4. Arrange half the kale leaves along the length of the parchment, forming a base to prevent the salmon skin from sticking. Set the salmon on top of the leaves, skin-side down. Lather the top side with oil and season thoroughly with the seasoning. Top the salmon with the lemon slices. Arrange the remaining kale leaves in a layer covering the salmon. Cover the salmon with a layer of parchment and another double layer of foil. Fold and enclose all the edges of the foil to seal the packet.

5. Add the salmon to the hot coals and cover the packet with more coals. Make sure it is covered in ashy low-heat coals as they will cook the salmon from the top down and bottom up. Cook for 8 to 10 minutes, or until the salmon reaches an internal temperature of about 145°F (63°C). Pull the salmon off the fire. Carefully open the foil and transfer the salmon to a platter to rest for 2 to 3 minutes. Discard the foil, parchment, and leaves.

6. To make the honey butter: Place a cast-iron skillet over the coals and add the butter and honey to melt. Pour the sauce over the salmon. Serve the salmon whole or cut into fillets.

HERB BUTTER OYSTERS ON THE HALF SHELL

If you have never cooked oysters on the grill, you are missing something special. Sure, it may not be for oyster purists. And, although grilled oysters are delicious, they are really for packing full of butter and seasoning. But, I say, if you want to leave a few oysters raw, go for it! Most of this recipe can be made hours ahead: Mix that delicious butter, scoop it onto the oyster meat, place in the fridge to firm, and cook it right on the coals when you're ready. It is as simple as that. As for the type of oyster, choose whatever is freshest!

PREP TIME: 45 MINUTES | SETTING TIME: 1 HOUR | COOK TIME: 10 MINUTES

4 servings

FOR HERB BUTTER

1 cup (224 g) unsalted butter, at room temperature

2 tablespoons (8 g) chopped fresh parsley

2 tablespoons (2 g) chopped fresh cilantro

1 tablespoon (4 g) chopped fresh oregano leaves

2 teaspoons sea salt

1 teaspoon chopped fresh chives

1 teaspoon fresh lemon juice

FOR OYSTERS

12 oysters, shucked

Lemon wedges, for garnish

Hot sauce, for garnish

FOR SPECIAL GEAR

Oyster shucker

Fire-resistant gloves

Large rock salt

1. To make the herb butter: In a large bowl, stir together all the herb butter ingredients. Set aside.

2. To make the oysters: Using a towel, cloth, or glove, place one oyster flat, cup-side up, between the cloth. Place and oyster shucker along the split opening of the shellfish. Gently insert and twist the blade. Once the shell splits open, move the shucker flat across the oyster and pull it open until one half of the shell is off. Discard the shell without the meat. Scoop underneath the meat with the shucker to cut it loose from the other half of the shell. Look for any cracked shell pieces and discard those, too. Set the oyster aside in its half shell and finish shucking the others.

3. Place a heaping tablespoonful (about 14 g) of butter on top of each shucked oyster shell. Refrigerate the buttered oysters for 1 hour to set.

4. Preheat your fire using the instructions for Cooking on the Coals (see page 33), bringing it to a medium-high temperature (about 375°F, or 190°C). Once ready to cook, blow over the coals to remove excess ash.

5. Pull the oysters out of the fridge right before you are ready to cook and place them right onto the coals. Cook for about 3 minutes to let the butter melt. Try to avoid flare-ups by placing the oysters level on the coals so the butter does not run off. Once the butter melts, pull the oysters off the using a fire-resistant glove. Let rest for 3 minutes to cool.

6. For serving, cover a plate or platter with rock salt and arrange the oysters on top. Serve with lemon wedges and hot sauce.

Cooking Vegetables on the Coals

You have learned to cook meat on the coals, but you can also cook tons of vegetables there, too. Hearty veggies are the ideal candidates for coal cooking, as they can handle the higher temperatures without becoming overly burnt. Here are a few ideas for coal-roasted vegetables to add when you are cooking on the coals:

Bell peppers: One of my favorite ways to make salsa (see Charred Salsa Verde, page 182) is by roasting the veggies over the coals before chopping them. This gives a distinct smoky flavor to the salsa while preserving the freshness. Coal-roasted bell peppers are the same idea. I love to add some whole peppers to the coals when making steaks as they are quick, easy, and delicious. Add the whole peppers and cook for 3 to 4 minutes, turning and rotating about every 30 seconds. Make a medley of sliced coal-roasted bell peppers with some fresh red onion for a versatile side.

Corn in its husk: Grilled corn is delicious, but coal-roasted corn is amazing. The biggest key is to soak the corn in water before cooking it, as you want it to steam inside the husk. Cooking the corn in its husk provides a protective barrier that keeps the kernels from burning. Serve with herb butter (see page 186) or a little of my Chipotle Rub (page 191) sprinkled on top.

Butternut squash: My wife's favorite thing to roast in the coals is butternut squash. This vegetable has a hardy skin that can withstand the coals' intensity. Cook for 1 to 2 hours on the coals until tender and soft in the middle. Once done, open it up and slice out the meat. Top with some butter, salt, and a little sugar for a nice sweet vegetable cooked on the coals.

SPICY LAMB CHOPS

The seasoning on these outstanding chops is an ode to one of my favorites: harissa. Hailing from North Africa, harissa is a complex mixture of spices and citrus. It is made for all kinds of cooking and is one of the most versatile seasonings I have found. It stands up to strong flavors, which is why I recommend it here, where you have both lamb and a lot of character from the coals.

PREP TIME: 15 MINUTES | COOK TIME: 10 MINUTES

2 servings

FOR SPICY PASTE

1½ tablespoons (12 g) chipotle powder or ancho chili powder

1½ tablespoons (12 g) serrano powder or red pepper flakes

1 tablespoon (8.4 g) sweet paprika or smoked paprika

2 teaspoons ground cumin

2 teaspoons sea salt

1 teaspoon caraway seeds

1 teaspoon coriander seeds

1 teaspoon garlic powder

¼ cup (60 ml) olive oil

1 tablespoon (15 ml) fresh lemon juice

FOR LAMB CHOPS

2 (6-bone) bone-in racks of lamb

Chopped fresh cilantro, for garnish

Lemon wedges, for garnish

1. To make the spicy paste: In a medium-size bowl, stir together the spices for the paste. Stir in the oil and lemon juice to form a paste, mixing thoroughly. Set aside.

2. To make the lamb chops: Using a sharp knife, cut between the bones of the racks of lamb to create lamb chops. Cut close to the side of the rib bone to glide past the bone between each chop. Place on a cutting board. Lather the spice paste on both sides of the chops.

3. Preheat your fire using the instructions for Cooking on the Coals (see page 33), bringing it to a medium-high temperature (about 375°F, or 190°C). When ready to cook, blow over the coals to get rid of any loose ash.

4. Add the lamb chops to the coals and cook for 1 minute, 30 seconds until the outside of the chops is charred. Flip the chops, brush off any coals or ash, and place them back on the coals. Cook for 1 minute, or until the lamb reaches an internal temperature of 145°F (63°C). Pull the chops off the fire and let rest for 5 minutes.

5. Plate the lamb chops, garnish with cilantro, and serve lemon wedges on the side for squeezing.

3
INDIRECT FIRE COOKING

Now that you are fully immersed in the world of direct fire cooking, it's time to discuss cooking over open fire *indirectly*, meaning the food will not be in direct contact with, immediately above, or touching something that is right above the fire, but, rather, away from it.

This is not an uncommon way of cooking—these cooking styles have been used for a very long time. Cooking food next to the fire using its radiant heat is an approach long practiced around the world for tough, fatty, and even delicate cuts of meat.

The place I like to start when discussing indirect cooking is hanging and leaning. Although these might be two different "styles," the process of using the fire is almost identical. By trussing your food with string and hanging it over the fire, it cooks slowly, soaking up lots of wood-fire flavor. Recipes like Hanging Chicken (page 104) or Hanging Prime Rib (page 112) are just the beginning here. In the same vein, leaning salmon on cedar planks or hanging whole lamb on an Asado cross accomplishes the same thing, just using different equipment.

Skewers and the rotisserie are old inventions finding relevance again. Cultures from North Africa to South America utilize skewers to slowly cook food next to a fire. Try recipes like Brazilian-Inspired Picanha (page 126) or Rotisserie Leg of Lamb (page 130) in the backyard. As long as you use real wood for authentic flavor, you can skewer these and cook indirectly for a flavor-packed result.

Finally, I offer a bit of barbecue. This is the low and slow cooking style I grew up with, but I still like trying out different techniques—my recipes for Smoked Pork Belly Burnt Ends (page 150) or Salt-Baked Red Snapper (page 146) are fun twists on traditional barbecue.

HANGING AND LEANING

The first stop on our indirect cooking journey is hanging and leaning. This style of cooking has roots in ancient, almost barbaric, techniques. For me, it is all about immersing myself in this style of thinking: How would my ancestors have cooked large cuts of meat or fish without the luxury of modern kitchens or technology?

Take, for example, the Hanging Chicken (page 104). If you join me on this one, we will truss a whole roaster chicken in my special style and cook it over the coals for 6 to 7 hours until done. So, the hanging aspect is just the device with which we slowly cook the chicken to render it tender and delicious.

As you flip through this section, you'll notice the recipes are all about low and slow cooking so the food absorbs as much smokiness as possible. So, don't skimp on the time it takes to cook the food. Be patient! The love and attention you give your food will be paid proportionately in the flavor of your dish.

Whole Lamb al Asador (page 109), an ode to the Gaucho cooking methods of South America, cooks for nearly 7 hours! That said, some other recipes do not take as long. You can make a holiday-style Hanging Prime Rib (page 112) hung right over the coals, in 2 to 3 hours, or the Leaning Salmon Plank with Lemon-Dill Sauce (page 101), which cooks for about 1½ hours.

For the salmon, nail it to a thick wood plank, using food-grade stainless-steel nails (yes, they do exist), and lean it against the fire for about 1 hour until done. It's such a simple recipe, but it's all about delicately cooking the fish until it's perfect. So, without further ado, let's get to that recipe right now!

LEANING SALMON PLANK WITH LEMON-DILL SAUCE

The simple salt, pepper, and garlic flavor on the salmon lets the smoke from the fire star as the main flavor in this plank recipe. Topped with a fresh lemon-dill sauce, it will be a true party showstopper that looks a lot more complicated than it is. You do need the right equipment. Getting a thick-cut untreated wood plank is essential, as is making sure it's thick enough to hold a nail. Cheaper or thinner wood planks split easily when you secure the nails. Make sure to use food-grade stainless-steel nails as well, avoiding any "treated" nails, as they are not meant to touch your food.

PREP TIME: 45 MINUTES | COOK TIME: 1 HOUR 20 MINUTES

8 servings

FOR LEMON-DILL SAUCE

½ cup (120 g) plain Greek yogurt

1 tablespoon (4 g) chopped fresh parsley

2 teaspoons fresh dill

1 teaspoon red pepper flakes

2 lemons

FOR SALMON

10 to 15 whole kale leaves

1 whole side of salmon (preferably king or sockeye), cleaned

2 to 3 teaspoons (15 ml) olive oil

1 tablespoon (18 g) kosher salt

1 tablespoon (6 g) black pepper

1 tablespoon (9 g) garlic powder

FOR SPECIAL GEAR

Large (2½- to 3-foot long × 1- to 2-inch-thick, or 75 to 90 cm long × 2.5 to 5 cm thick) untreated wood plank (preferably oak or hickory)

Food-grade 304 stainless-steel nails or any untreated nail

NOTE: Avoid galvanized or any painted nail as it is not food safe can discolor your food.

Hammer

Heat-resistant glove

1. To make the lemon-dill sauce: In a medium-size bowl, whisk the yogurt, parsley, dill, and red pepper flakes to combine.

2. Grate the zest of 2 lemons into the bowl, then juice them into the bowl. Whisk thoroughly. Cover and refrigerate until serving.

3. To make the salmon: Preheat your fire using the instructions for the Hanging and Leaning method (see page X), bringing it to a medium-high temperature (about 375°F, or 190°C).

recipe continues

4. Place the wood plank on a flat surface and lay the kale leaves along it to make a bed for the salmon.

5. Place the salmon, skin-side down, directly on the kale. Lather the salmon in oil, then season with salt, pepper, and garlic powder.

6. Using 6 to 8 stainless-steel nails, nail the fish to the plank. Start in the top left corner, about 1 inch (2.5 cm) from the fish's edge so you nail a meatier part. Carefully hammer the nail into the board so it does not split—but you do not need the nail to go all the way through the board. We want the nails sticking out a bit so we can easily pull them out once the fish is done. Once the first nail is firmly in place, continue along both sides of the fish and add a nail every 3 inches (7.5 cm). When the fish is secure, hold it up to make sure it does not slide down the plank, or that any nails come loose. Fix any issues.

7. Using whatever resource you have (rocks, bricks, post) for support, lean your salmon at an almost 90 degree angle about 2 to 2½ feet (60 to 75 cm) from the fire with the head (wider part) pointing toward the ground and the salmon facing the fire. Cook the salmon this way for about 20 minutes. Feed the fire, as needed, to maintain a consistent temperature. Once you notice a change in color and caramelization, you'll know the fish is cooking.

   After 20 minutes, rotate the fish so the tail points to the ground. Continue cooking for 20 minutes at the same temperature.

   Lean the plank on its side so the belly meat is close to the ground and closer to the fire. Cook for 10 minutes.

   Lastly, rotate the fish so the spine side cooks for 10 minutes. Once the fish is caramelized all over, check the internal temperature. It is done when it reaches 145°F (63°C). Pull it off the fire and let rest for 5 minutes.

8. After resting, lay the plank flat and use a heat-resistant glove to carefully pull out the nails. Dispose of the used nails.

9. To serve, top the whole salmon with the lemon-dill and serve directly from the plank.

HANGING CHICKEN

I'm not going to lie to you and say this one is easy; this recipe is one of the more intense cooks to master. It takes patience and consistency, like smoking a brisket or cooking Whole Lamb al Asador (page 109). The reward is one of the best chickens you have ever tasted, but the price is keeping a consistent fire going while preventing the chicken from burning. This recipe achieves flavor two ways—using a citrus spice rub as well as a nice beer brine. But none of those flavors takes over, as this chicken is all about the char from cooking over the fire. My biggest tip for this cook is to grab a bunch of beer, bring the cooler next to the chicken, and watch the chicken closely. Enjoy the process. Oh, and sides like rice and beans pair perfectly and can be made ahead of time, letting you focus on the chicken.

PREP TIME: 30 MINUTES | COOK TIME: 5 TO 6 HOURS

4 servings

FOR CHICKEN

1 whole roaster chicken (preferably a smaller chicken; it cooks faster)

2 tablespoons (36 g) kosher salt

2 tablespoons (12 g) black pepper

1 tablespoon (8.4 g) sweet paprika

2 teaspoons cayenne pepper

Grated zest of 1 lemon

Juice of 1 lemon

1½ tablespoons (23 ml) olive oil

FOR SIMPLE BASTING BRINE

1 (12-ounce, or 360 ml) bottle beer, white wine, or water

6 garlic cloves, peeled

2 tablespoons (36 g) kosher salt

Grated zest of 1 lemon

Juice of 1 lemon

FOR SPECIAL GEAR

Butcher's twine

Tripod or something to hang the chicken from

1. To make the chicken: To start, we need to truss the chicken. Cut a 6-foot (180 cm) piece of butcher's twine and soak it in water for 15 minutes so it will not burn during the cook.

2. Place the chicken on a work surface, breast-side up. Position the string underneath the back of the legs so it is at the mid-back of the chicken, with the chicken in the middle of the string. Cross the string across the middle of the chicken (around the middle of the legs) and pull hard so the legs are pushed up slightly. Wrap the string once around the bottom of the leg bones, starting from the outside then going around toward the inside. Then, while keeping pressure so the string does not loosen, bring both ends of the string over the neck and back around the tail until you are at the cross point where you started. Make sure the string is very tight on the chicken and tie it off in the middle. Cross the strings underneath your cross point and tie them off tightly.

3. In a small food-safe bowl, stir together the salt, black pepper, paprika, and cayenne.

recipe continues

How to Truss a Chicken

Trussing a chicken is hugely important to a successful cook because it holds the chicken together tightly for cooking and gives us a way to hang it over the fire without ruining the meat. Trussing chicken for hanging is simple and quick. I have used multiple techniques, but this is my favorite:

1. Cut a length of string about 6 feet (180 cm) long.
2. Lay the chicken, breast-side up, on the string in the middle of it.
3. Cross the string over the top of the legs tightly.
4. Wrap the string from the outside in and around the drumstick and pull it tight.
5. Fully wrap the two ends of the string up over the head, back down the spine, and under the tail until you are back where you started.
6. Tie the string underneath your cross point and secure it.

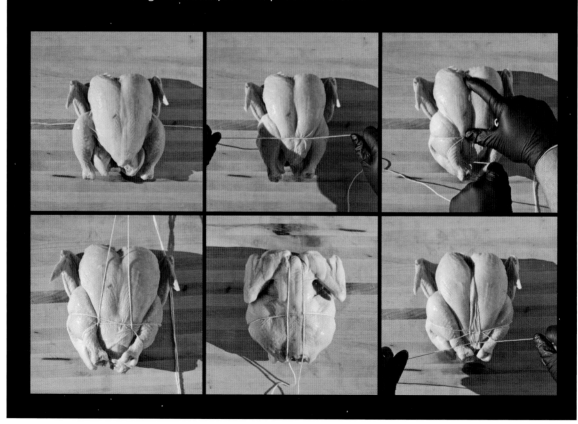

4. In another small bowl, stir together the lemon zest, lemon juice, and oil. Lather the outside of the chicken in the lemon oil, then season thoroughly with the spices. Cover the chicken and refrigerate for 1 hour.

5. Preheat your fire using the instructions for the Hanging and Leaning method (see page 37), bringing it to a medium-high temperature (about 375°F, or 190°C).

6. To make the simple basting brine: Place a heatproof pot over the flames and add the beer and garlic. Bring to a boil and cook for 3 minutes. Add the salt, lemon zest, and lemon juice. Continue cooking for 2 to 3 minutes. Transfer to a heatproof bowl to use while cooking the chicken.

7. Pull the chicken from the refrigerator and let it come to room temperature. Uncover it.

8. Set up your hanging device directly over the coals with a string or metal chain suspended from it. Safely, using your hand, check the temperature of the fire by placing it 6 inches (15 cm) from the heat. Wherever you can safely hold your hand for 7 to 8 seconds without pulling it away is where you should begin cooking the chicken. Remember, add wood and coals, as needed, to maintain a consistent temperature throughout the cook.

9. Place the chicken on the hanging device, breast-side facing the fire. Cook the chicken like this for about 1½ hours, basting with the beer brine every 30 to 45 minutes.

10. Rotate the chicken so the back side faces the heat and cook for 1½ hours, basting with the beer brine every 30 to 45 minutes.

11. Place the chicken with the legs facing the flames and cook for 1½ hours, basting with the beer brine every 30 to 45 minutes.

12. Lastly, hang the chicken with the neck and breast facing the flames for the last 1 to 1½ hours of cooking, basting with the beer brine every 30 to 45 minutes. Watch for the chicken burning. To prevent this, raise it from the heat and rotate it to another side.

13. Once the chicken reaches an internal temperature of 165°F (74°C) at the thickest part, and all over, it is safe to pull it off the fire. Let rest for 5 minutes. For serving, halve the chicken, or cut it into 8 pieces.

WHOLE LAMB AL ASADOR

One of the holy grails for fire cooking is whole lamb al Asador, which is the traditional Spanish name for this dish. While this is a large cook to tackle, it is a staple in the hall of fame for fire cooking. What follows is my path for you to make the lamb al Asador pilgrimage. Delicious and fresh, this lamb features citrus and herbs along with a hit of vinegar to cut through the fat. Just make sure to secure the lamb well to your Asador cross, as it tends to bow once it becomes tender. Also, don't be afraid to double the brine. There is enough to get through the cook as written, but if you are a liberal baster or your cook goes longer, you want to keep the brine going strong the whole time.

PREP TIME: 1 HOUR 30 MINUTES | COOK TIME: 6 HOURS 30 MINUTES

12 servings

FOR LAMB

1 whole lamb, butterflied by your butcher

1½ cups (384 g) sea salt

½ cup (32 g) chopped fresh parsley

BEER BASTING BRINE

1 white onion, cubed

2 lemons, halved

2 bay leaves

12 garlic cloves, unpeeled

3 (12-ounce, or 360 ml) bottles of your favorite beer

1 cup (240 ml) white wine vinegar

¼ cup (60 ml) olive oil

2 tablespoons (36 g) kosher salt

2 tablespoons (11.2 g) red pepper flakes

FOR SPECIAL GEAR

Handsaw (optional)

Food-safe metal wiring

Wire cutters

Metal Asado cross

Large cast-iron skillet

Large barbecue basting mop

1. To make the lamb: If your lamb did not come butterflied, we can easily do this ourselves. Line a large, sturdy table with parchment paper and place the lamb on it. Grab a handsaw and begin splitting the spine in half. I recommend starting at the top of the spine and splitting from there down to the end of the ribs. Once the lamb begins to give way, carefully pull it open so the inside rib meat becomes exposed and the lamb can lay flat. Keep cutting until the whole lamb lies flat, turning it cut-side (bone-side) down.

2. Using a good filet knife, trim any excess fat off the lamb, mostly from the back and middle of the cavity.

3. Whether you butterflied the lamb yourself or it came that way, score the back-side fat in a crosshatch pattern (if it has not already been done) and season the lamb inside and out with salt.

recipe continues

4. Using food-safe metal wire and wire cutters, secure the butterflied lamb to the Asado cross. Using a long thin knife, carefully poke 2 holes at the middle of the spine, on both sides and right next to it. Thread a piece of metal wire through the holes and secure it to the back of the cross (try to get it through a hole in the cross if possible). Repeat this process at another part of the spine to keep the lamb from bowing out while cooking. Make sure to secure the legs as well to prevent bowing.

5. Preheat your fire using the instructions for the Hanging and Leaning method (see page 37), bringing it to a medium-high temperature (about 375°F, or 190°C).

6. Lean the lamb over the fire with the inside toward the fire first. Cook at a consistent medium-high temperature for 3 hours. The lamb should begin to caramelize, turning reddish brown, and become tender. If the fire is too hot, move the lamb farther away from it.

7. To make the beer basting brine: As the lamb begins to cooks, in a cast-iron skillet, combine all the basting brine ingredients. Set the skillet next to the fire and simmer for 10 minutes to blend the flavors. Baste the lamb all over every 30 minutes to maintain moisture.

8. After 3 hours, carefully rotate the lamb so its back is toward the fire. Continue to cook the lamb for another 3 hours, basting every 30 minutes to maintain moisture, until the internal temperature reaches 185°F (85°C). Once the lamb is completely reddish brown in color and its internal temperature is correct, pull it off the fire and let rest for 10 minutes.

9. Using a carving knife, begin carving the lamb by removing the legs and slicing them (See Rotisserie Leg of Lamb, page 130, for slicing instructions). Remove the ribs and enjoy the tenderloin right next to the spine. All other meat can be pulled off or sliced off as needed. Serve the lamb garnished with fresh parsley.

HANGING PRIME RIB

The ultimate family dinner is prime rib—a massive rib eye to feed a crowd. For my take on this classic, we treat it with style, hanging it over the fire, of course. This recipe is straightforward, requiring trussing, seasoning, and cooking over the coals. I usually let my prime rib cook for about 2½ hours before I pull it off the fire. I recommend a simple seasoning: salt, pepper, and garlic. The crispy ends of the meat caramelize so well that it gives off a sweet yet savory flavor all its own. Serve it with Creamy Horseradish Sauce, which gets its spice with a hit of hot sauce in addition to horseradish—double the recipe if you really like horseradish sauce! You can also try this recipe with boneless prime rib (trussing it really well) or a whole New York strip roast.

PREP TIME: 30 MINUTES | COOK TIME: 2 HOURS 30 MINUTES

8 servings

1 (3- to 4-bone) prime rib roast

2 tablespoons (30 ml) olive oil

2 tablespoons (36 g) kosher salt

2 tablespoons (12 g) black pepper

2 tablespoons (18 g) garlic powder

1 recipe Creamy Horseradish Sauce (page 185), chilled

FOR SPECIAL GEAR

Butcher's twine

S hook

1. Cut a 6-foot (180 cm) piece of butcher's twine and soak it in water for 15 minutes to prevent it from burning and snapping during the cook.

2. Place the roast on a cutting board, bone-side up. Place the twine underneath the middle of the prime rib lengthwise so the roast is in the center of the length of string. Wrap the string up over the top of the prime rib and cross the strings. Secure the tie and flip the roast over. Take the two loose ends of string and cross them over the top of the roast again so you now have a fully encased steak. Repeat this 2 or 3 more times until you have a very securely tied prime rib that can handle a couple hours cooking over the fire. Wrap aluminum foil over the ends of the bones to prevent burning, if you like.

3. Preheat your fire using the instructions for the Hanging and Leaning method (see page 37), bringing it to a medium-high temperature (about 375°F, or 190°C).

4. Lather the roast with oil and season all over with the salt, pepper, and garlic powder. Set aside.

5. Set up your hanging device directly over the coals with a string or metal chain suspended from it. Safely using your hand, check the temperature of the fire by placing it 6 inches (15 cm) from the heat. Wherever you can safely hold your hand for 7 to 8 seconds without pulling it away is where you should begin cooking. Remember to add wood, as needed, to keep a consistent temperature and rotate the meat if it begins to burn.

recipe continues

6. Secure the roast to the hanging device, bone-side facing the heat. Cook for 45 minutes. Flip the roast so the bones face away the heat and cook for 45 minutes more. Finally, hang the prime rib so one side faces the heat. Cook for about 30 minutes. Turn the roast so the opposite side faces the heat and cook for 30 minutes more. Rotate the prime rib to sear off any sides that are not fully cooked. Once the prime rib reaches an internal temperature of 120°F (49°C) at its thickest point, pull it off the fire and let rest for 30 minutes.

7. Pull the horseradish sauce from the refrigerator.

8. Remove the trussing twine and thinly slice the roast. Top with the horseradish sauce and enjoy!

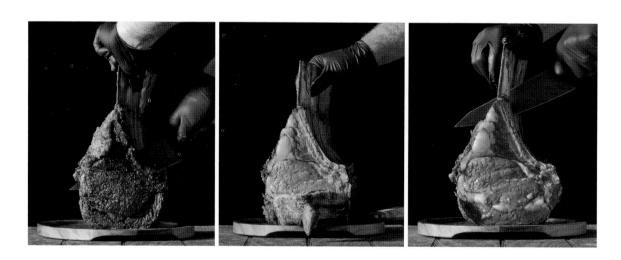

CHARRED AND GLAZED PINEAPPLE

If you have a fire going and the main event is one of the meat recipes we've already cooked, adding this to the cook is a no-brainer. It's a bonus dish that I think pairs so well with chicken, pork, and even beef that I usually cook a few of these pineapples every time we do big fire-cooking dinners.

This recipe is an ode to the great Francis Mallmann, and the key to making these is getting that fire vertical (see page 37). Because the pineapple hangs lengthwise next to the fire, you need to have the heat coming at it from the side, not the bottom. This helps caramelize the fruit everywhere, which is the best part, next to the honey butter glaze.

PREP TIME: 20 MINUTES | COOK TIME: 20 MINUTES

8 servings

FOR PINEAPPLE

1 whole pineapple

2 tablespoons (30 g) light brown sugar

2 teaspoons ground cinnamon

2 teaspoons sea salt

FOR HONEY BUTTER GLAZE

¼ cup (80 g) honey

2 tablespoons (28 g) unsalted butter

FOR SPECIAL GEAR:

Butcher's twine

Cast-iron skillet

S hook

1. To make the pineapple: Carefully slice off the outside skin of the pineapple, while not shaving off too much pineapple meat. Leave the pineapple crown attached.

2. In a small food-safe bowl, stir together the brown sugar, cinnamon, and salt. Thoroughly season the outside of the pineapple with the spices. Refrigerate the fruit to rest until you are ready to cook.

3. Preheat your fire using the instructions for the Hanging and Leaning method (see page 37), bringing it to a medium-high temperature (about 375°F, or 190°C).

4. Set up your hanging device next to the fire with a string or metal chain suspended from it. Safely using your hand, check the temperature of the fire by placing it 6 inches (15 cm) from the heat. Wherever you can safely hold your hand for 7 to 8 seconds without pulling it away is where you should begin cooking. Make sure the fire is vertical so it cooks the pineapple from top to bottom.

5. Cut a 3-foot (90 cm) piece of butcher's twine and soak it in water for 15 minutes to prevent it from burning and snapping during the cook.

6. Wrap and tie the end of the butcher's twine around the base of the pineapple crown. Using the rest of the butcher's twine, hang the pineapple next to the fire. Cook the pineapple for about 20 minutes until it caramelizes and becomes tender.

recipe continues

7. To make the honey butter glaze: While the pineapple cooks, preheat a skillet next to the fire near low heat. Carefully add the honey and butter to the skillet. Let simmer for 2 minutes to blend near low heat so the glaze does not burn. Pull it off the fire and keep warm.

8. Once tender, pull the pineapple off the fire and let rest for 2 minutes.

9. For serving, shave the pineapple into slivers, drizzle the glaze over top, and enjoy!

Different Materials for Hanging

While I truss just about any protein in butcher's twine, there are some different materials that I use for hanging foods. Each has its pros and cons, but they all serve a purpose. Let's look at the options:

x **Butcher's twine:** This is the classic string that I use to truss chicken (see sidebar, page 106) or prime rib. It is readily available at most grocery or cooking stores. It is also decently strong after you soak it in water. That said, it can break easily if exposed to too much heat. It is also not the most adjustable string for cooks that need lots of up or down movement. In the end, I recommend using butcher's twine for hanging only if you do not have access to flexible wire or metal chains.

x **Flexible wire:** Using flexible wire is a good choice when cooking over fire. It is extremely durable and can hold a decent amount of weight and it is adjustable. Twist or untwist the wire, as needed, to move your food up or down. That said, be careful about the type of flexible wire you use. I recommend food-grade stainless-steel flexible wire, as anything else is not meant for fire cooking. It's difficult to find at times, so use it when readily available. Look for it at most home and garden stores, or online.

x **Metal chains:** The readily available and ideal material for hanging food is metal chain. You can easily attach S hooks to the chain where needed and it is relatively simple to adjust for height. You can also easily find chains able to handle the high intensity of fire cooking. Use a food-grade butcher's hook at the end of the chain to attach your food.

SKEWERS

Cooking with skewers, or on the rotisserie, is my bread and butter. It is one of my favorite ways to cook over fire because of this simple fact: nothing is between the coals and my food.

Okay, it's true. Skewers can be used with both indirect and direct heat. However, most of the time that I cook with skewers, I use them indirectly so a good crust develops on the food and so I do not lose too much juice from a piece of meat to the coals.

Cooking with skewers, or on a rotisserie, is not a brand-new concept. In fact, I hope you are starting to see that most of these cooking techniques are not new but, rather, becoming popular again as we look back to the successful ways humans cooked before the era of the propane tank. (Some are just like the mullet or plaid shirts, which come in and out of fashion!)

This cooking style opens a lot of doors that other ways of cooking do not. Since you are skewering your meat, you have better access to it for basting, seasoning, and flavor on the food because the entire outside surface is exposed to the fire (versus just one side being pointed toward it). Take, for example, Rotisserie Leg of Lamb (page X). I marinate the meat overnight while reserving some marinade for basting the next day. While the leg cooks, I slather the entire outside in marinade.

Or how about the Brazilian-Inspired Picanha (page 126)? A whole cut of picanha steak is seared off, sliced into filets, skewered, and thrown over a low flame. It will cook long enough to soak up all the smokiness yet retain all the juiciness. Truly epic.

But let's start with some simple Al Pastor Skewered Tacos (following). This is a fun little twist on skewers by throwing in a *trompo*-styled vertical spit you can easily make at home. Need I say more?

AL PASTOR SKEWERED TACOS

We are going to kick off this section by crushing some al pastor tacos. If you have never heard of al pastor, it is a quintessential taco from Mexico that carries all kinds of flavor: savory, sweet, sour, and spicy. Top this taco with some Charred Salsa Verde (page 182) while you are at it!

PREP TIME: 1 HOUR | MARINATING TIME: 4 HOURS | COOK TIME: 3 HOURS

8 servings

FOR PORK

1 (5-pound or 2.27 kg kg) whole boneless pork shoulder

2 onions, quartered, plus more as needed

FOR AL PASTOR MARINADE

1 whole pineapple

1 tablespoon (15 ml) olive oil

12 garlic cloves, minced

1 teaspoon dried oregano

1 teaspoon ground cumin

1 teaspoon ground cinnamon

1 teaspoon black pepper

½ cup (80 g) diced white onion

½ cup (120 ml) pineapple juice

¼ cup (60 ml) distilled white vinegar

2 tablespoons (36 g) kosher salt

2 tablespoons (34 g) chipotle peppers in adobo sauce

2 tablespoons (44 g) achiote paste

FOR SERVING

Corn or flour tortillas

Chopped fresh cilantro

Diced pineapple

Diced white onion

Lime wedges

FOR SPECIAL GEAR

Cast-iron skillet

6- to 8-inch (15 to 30 cm)-long wooden skewers, soaked in water overnight

1. To make the pork: Place the pork on a clean work surface. Using a very sharp knife, carefully slice the pork shoulder into thin, ¼-inch (0.6 cm) pieces, and return to the refrigerator. Clean up.

2. To make the al pastor marinade: Cut off the top crown and base of the pineapple and refrigerate for later use. Cut half the pineapple meat into cubes for the marinade and dice the remaining pineapple for the taco garnish.

3. Preheat your fire using the instructions for the Skillet method (see page 30), bringing it to a medium-high temperature (about 375°F, or 190°C).

4. In a skillet, combine the oil and garlic. Place the skillet between the 2 fire zones and cook for 2 minutes. Add the oregano, cumin, cinnamon, and pepper. Cook for 1 minute. Stir in the onion, pineapple juice, vinegar, pineapple cubes, salt, chipotles in adobo, and achiote paste. Bring to a simmer. Pull from the fire and let cool. Transfer to a blender and blend until liquefied. Pour the marinade through a strainer set over a bowl to remove any big pieces until you end up with a smooth marinade.

recipe continues

5. In a large food-safe container, place your largest pork slice and cover with a little marinade. Repeat until all the pork slices are in the container. Refrigerate to marinate for 4 hours or, ideally, overnight.

6. Preheat your fire using the instructions for the Skewer/Rotisserie method (see page 40), bringing it to a medium temperature (about 325°F, or 170°C).

7. Remove the pineapple crown and base from the refrigerator along with the pork. Using 2 wooden skewers, push up through the bottom of the pineapple base. Layer 1 one slice of marinating pork on top of another through the skewers over the base until all meat is on.

8. Place the pineapple crown on top of the pork and insert 2 or 3 wooden skewers through it for added support. Place the skewered meat and pineapple in a cast-iron skillet. Add more skewers, as needed, and the onion to help support and balance the food.

9. Place the skillet with the skewered meat over indirect heat on the grill. Close the lid and cook for 3 hours, or until the middle of the meat registers at 165°F (74°C). Rotate the skillet to cook all sides of the meat evenly and add more charcoal or wood chunks to the fire, as needed, to maintain a consistent temperature. The meat is close to done when it is deep orange in color with nice charred parts on the outside. Pull the skillet off the grill and let rest for 30 minutes.

10. To serve the tacos: Slice the meat vertically and place on a warm tortilla with cilantro, diced pineapple, diced onion, and lime wedges for squeezing.

BACON-WRAPPED MAPLE-BOURBON CHICKEN SKEWERS

If you're like me, you were excited about this recipe from the word "bacon." But wait, it also includes maple and bourbon? Come on! But there are some downsides. For one, this recipe title is a mouthful and cooking it requires precision. If you don't cook this totally indirect—if it catches even a small amount of direct heat—you risk burning the bacon and the chicken turning out overcooked on the outside and undercooked inside. But when cooked over the ideal indirect fire, it can't be beat. The chicken will be perfectly cooked and you get to glaze and caramelize the bacon directly over the coals at the end.

PREP TIME: 45 MINUTES | COOK TIME: 35 MINUTES

6 servings

FOR BARBECUE SEASONING

1½ tablespoons (23 g) light brown sugar

1 tablespoon (8.4 g) smoked paprika

1 tablespoon (6.9 g) onion powder

1 tablespoon (18 g) kosher salt

1 tablespoon (6 g) black pepper

1 teaspoon ground cinnamon

FOR CHICKEN

2 pounds (908 g) boneless, skinless chicken breast, cut into 2-inch (5 cm) cubes

2 tablespoons (30 ml) olive oil

10 to 12 thin-cut bacon slices, halved widthwise

FOR MAPLE-BOURBON GLAZE

¼ cup (60 ml) bourbon

¼ cup (80 g) maple syrup

2 tablespoons (28 g) unsalted butter

FOR SPECIAL GEAR

24-inch (60 cm)-long large skewers

Basting skillet

Basting brush

1. To make the barbecue seasoning: In a small food-safe bowl, stir together all the seasoning ingredients. Set aside.

2. To make the chicken: Place the chicken cubes in a medium-size food-safe bowl. Lather the chicken with oil and thoroughly coat with the barbecue season. Refrigerate the chicken for 30 minutes to 1 hour.

3. Pull the chicken from the refrigerator. Wrap each chicken cube in ½ bacon slice and place on a skewer. For a more secure skewer, thread the chicken onto the skewer through the loose end of the bacon to keep the bacon secure. Thread all the chicken pieces and set the skewers aside.

4. Preheat your fire using the instructions for the Skewer/Rotisserie method (see page 40), bringing it to a medium temperature (about 325°F, or 170°C).

recipe continues

5. Place the skewers on the cooler side of the grill and cook for about 35 minutes, rotating the skewers every 7 to 8 minutes to ensure an even cook, until the chicken reaches an internal temperature of 165°F (74°C). Watch for flare-ups from the bacon. Move the skewers away from the fire if the bacon begins to burn or flare. While the chicken cooks, make the maple bourbon glaze.

6. To make the maple-bourbon glaze: After 15 minutes of cooking, preheat a basting skillet over direct heat. Carefully add the bourbon to the skillet and simmer for 2 to 3 minutes. Pull the skillet off direct heat and add the maple syrup and butter. Stir until smooth.

7. During the last 5 minutes of cooking, move the chicken skewers over direct heat. Carefully lather the glaze over the chicken to caramelize the bacon. Cook for only 30 seconds per side, glazing constantly, until the outside is crispy and amber in color. Once done glazing, pull the skewers off the fire and let rest for 5 minutes.

8. Serve the chicken on the skewers or pull the chicken off and plate. Either way, add a little extra glaze to the chicken.

BRAZILIAN-INSPIRED PICANHA

If you are an avid griller, you might be familiar with this superb cut of beef that, in South America, is called picanha. If not, then I have a treat for you. Picanha is a delicious hearty cut hailing from the back side of the animal commonly called the round. What makes picanha so enticing is its fat cap—no, you do not want to carve off that fat! It gives this cut of meat its rich, savory flavor. Pair this dish with a side of chimichurri to cut through that rich fat. Pro tip: When shopping for this cut of meat, ask your butcher for sirloin cap or whole rump cap.

PREP TIME: 25 MINUTES | COOK TIME: 1 HOUR

4 servings

1 (4-pound, or 1.8 kg) whole picanha, including fat cap

2 tablespoons (30 ml) olive oil, divided

3 tablespoons (54 g) coarse sea salt

2 tablespoons (18 g) garlic powder

1 recipe Classic Chimichurri (page 179)

FOR SPECIAL GEAR:

1 (24-inch, or 60 cm) large skewer

1. Preheat your fire using the instructions for Grilling (see page 29), bringing it to a medium-high temperature (about 375°F, or 190°C). Add the grill grate 5 minutes before cooking.

2. Lather the outside of the picanha with 1 tablespoon (15 ml) of oil and season with 1½ tablespoons (27 g) of salt and 1 tablespoon (9 g) of garlic powder. Refrigerate to rest for 5 minutes.

3. Once your grill is hot, sear the outside of the picanha, starting fat-cap down. Cook for 1 to 2 minutes until the fat cap has reduced by almost half. Note: Be aware of flare-ups caused by the fat and fire mixing. Pull off the picanha and cover the grill with a lid if necessary. Flip the picanha and sear all other sides of the steak for about 30 seconds per side. Once seared, pull the meat off the fire and transfer to a cutting board, placing it so the tail (small, thinner end) is pointed to your right-hand side.

4. Using a sharp knife, slice vertically down the picanha in 1½-inch (3.5 cm) segments to make steaks. Once you get to the tail, slice off the end piece and set aside to grill later. Lather the picanha steaks with the remaining 1 tablespoon (15 ml) of oil and season with the remaining 1½ tablespoons (27 g) of salt and 1 tablespoon (9 g) of garlic powder.

recipe continues

5. Curve the picanha steaks so they make a "C" shape by cupping them in your hand with the fat-cap side on the outside of the "C" shape. Line them up from biggest to smallest on your cutting board. One by one, skewer them so the unseared side faces out.

6. Revive your fire using the instructions for the Skewer/Rotisserie method (see page 40), bringing it to a medium temperature (about 325°F, or 170°C), adding more coals, if needed.

7. Place your skewered picanha onto the grill over indirect heat. Cook in 5-minute segments turning after each, for about 45 minutes total until the internal temperature of the steaks reaches 120°F (49°C) for medium-rare. Pull the steaks off the fire and let rest for 10 minutes.

8. To serve, carve small slices of the steak off the skewer, or pull off the steak and serve whole with a side of chimichurri for dipping.

What is Picanha?

The average American is unfamiliar with picanha. When I first started my fire-cooking journey, this was one of the prized cuts I wanted to cook. Funny thing was, I had already seen and eaten picanha at Brazilian steakhouses without knowing it.

Picanha is a cut of beef that comes from the rump of the cow. The rump is a portion of the upper back, which is also called the round in American butchery (there are different butchery breakdowns and names depending on the country). It can sometimes be called top sirloin cap, rump cap, or culotte. I recommend going to a full-breakdown butcher for this cut, as most grocery stores may not have access to that part of the cow.

This meat cut is extremely popular in Brazilian grilling, where it is traditionally sliced, skewered/grilled, and cooked over the coals until perfect. It is traditionally seasoned just with salt and sometimes served with a side of chimichurri. That said, you are welcome to experiment by using salt, garlic, pepper, or anything else you love on your steak.

One of the biggest questions I get about this cut is, "Do you eat the fat?" The answer: If you like fat, yes! The fat on this cut is almost like butter. The meat of picanha does not have a ton of intermuscular fat, so most of the flavor comes from the fat cap. It is similar in texture to sirloin with a perfect fat cap right at the end. If you are not a fat person, give the fat to someone who enjoys it!

ROTISSERIE LEG OF LAMB

A good leg of lamb grilled over hot flames is something you cannot beat for flavor. It's like a perfect blend of the heartiness of prime rib with the tenderness of filet mignon. The biggest key to making this meal delicious is the marinade. Carve out a whole night to let this lamb leg marinate as it will absolutely reflect in the tenderness and flavor of the meat. Everything's better with garlic, which really anchors this marinade. Mix that with delicious herbs in a sauce that will caramelize as you cook, and you have a winner.

PREP TIME: 30 MINUTES | MARINATING TIME: 4 HOURS | COOK TIME: 2 HOURS

8 servings

1 whole leg of lamb
(preferably bone-in)

1 white onion, cubed

8 garlic cloves, pressed or
minced

¼ cup (60 g) Dijon mustard

¼ cup (60 ml) white wine

3 tablespoons (45 ml)
olive oil

2 tablespoons (36 g)
kosher salt

2 tablespoons (6 g)
dried oregano

2 tablespoons (8 g) fresh
parsley, chopped

1 tablespoon (5.6 g) red
pepper flakes

Grated zest of 2 lemons

Juice of 2 lemons

FOR SPECIAL GEAR
Rotisserie

Basting brush

1. Using a sharp knife, score the outside layer of the leg of lamb only ¼ inch (0.6 cm) deep in a crosshatch on both the front and back of the leg. Place the leg in a food-safe marinating bin (ideally glass, not aluminum).

2. In a blender, combine the onion, garlic, mustard, wine, oil, salt, oregano, parsley, red pepper flakes, lemon zest, and lemon juice. Process until almost smooth. Reserve and refrigerate ¼ cup (60 ml) of marinade for basting. Pour the remaining marinade onto the lamb covering it thoroughly. Refrigerate the lamb to marinate for at least 4 hours or, ideally, overnight. About halfway through the marinating time, flip the lamb to help the marinade reach all sides of the meat.

3. Preheat your fire using the instructions for the Skewer/Rotisserie method (see page 40), bringing it to a medium temperature (about 325°F, or 170°C).

4. Pull the lamb leg out of the refrigerator and carefully skewer it onto the rotisserie. Secure the leg using side skewers to prevent it from coming loose on the rotisserie.

5. Place the leg of lamb over the fire and cook for about 1 hour. Retrieve the reserved marinade. Cook the lamb for 1 hour more, slowly slathering the lamb every 15 minutes with the reserved marinade until the sauce is gone and the thickest part of the meat reaches an internal temperature of 145°F (63°C). The lamb should begin to caramelize slowly while cooking. Watch for any burning or high heat as you might need to move the fire around to prevent that. Once the lamb leg reaches its ideal temperature, pull it off the fire, cover, and let rest for about 20 minutes.

recipe continues

6. Lay the leg on a cutting board on its side and thinly slice the meat on either side of the bone. Keep slicing until you reach bone. Next, lay the lamb flat, sliced-side down. Cut slices off the top of the leg until you reach bone, then slice all the way down the leg and guide your back parallel with the bone to cut the vertical slices into servings. Cut any remaining meat from the bone to be saved for later. Place the slices on a large platter and dig in!

Low and Slow versus Hot and Fast

Cooking with skewers, or on the rotisserie, is my bread and butter. It is one of my favorite ways to cook over fire because of this simple fact: nothing is between the coals and my food.

x **Cooking temperature:** Low and slow leans toward lower cooking temperatures, between 200°F and 250°F (93°C and 121°C). Hot and fast leans into slightly higher temperatures, between 275°F and 325°F (135°C and 163°C).

x **Cooking time:** The biggest difference is the time it takes to cook food using these two methods. Low and slow can take from 6 to 12 hours, depending on the cut. Hot and fast will cook the same meat in about half the time. This can appeal to people who are not interested in a 12-hour brisket—but there is some sacrifice.

x **Overall presentation:** One big tradeoff for low and slow versus hot and fast is presentation. Most hot and fast foods lack that distinctive smoke ring. They also have the potential to dry out, which you can combat with spritzing and watching your temperature.

In the end, low and slow is a tried-and-true method for those willing to take the time to do it. Hot and fast is a great option for quality results that is becoming more popular among fire cooks!

SPICY ROTISSERIE BEEF RIBS

Delicious dino ribs are classic beef plate ribs, which you can find at your local butcher, well-stocked grocery store, or online. If you struggle to find them, try this recipe with English—style beef ribs, which are the same as beef plate ribs except cut into smaller pieces. This recipe is not overly spicy, but it does pack tons of flavor. A nice smokiness comes from the chipotle powder, which is backed up with the aromas of garlic and onion. The seasoning will take on a lot of caramelization from the fire, so expect a nice outer crust once you're done cooking.

PREP TIME: 30 MINUTES | MARINATING TIME: 1 HOUR | COOK TIME: 5 HOURS

6 servings

FOR BEEF RIBS

2 whole bone-in beef plate ribs

2 tablespoons (30 ml) olive oil

FOR SEASONING

3 tablespoons (22.5 g) chipotle powder

2 tablespoons (36 g) kosher salt

2 tablespoons (12 g) black pepper

2 tablespoons (18 g) garlic powder

1 tablespoon (6.9 g) onion powder

1 tablespoon (12.5 g) sugar

2 teaspoons dried parsley flakes

FOR SPECIAL GEAR

Rotisserie

24-inch (60 cm) rotisserie skewers

1. To make the beef ribs: Place the beef plate ribs on a cutting board, bone-side down. Score the top fat cap with a ¼-inch (0.6 cm)-deep crosshatch pattern. Lather the ribs with oil.

2. To make the seasoning: In a medium-size bowl, stir together the seasoning ingredients. Thoroughly season the beef ribs all over with the spice mix. Refrigerate the ribs for at least 1 hour or, ideally, overnight.

3. Preheat your fire using the instructions for the Skewer/Rotisserie method (see page 40), bringing it to a medium temperature (about 325°F, or 170°C).

4. Time to skewer the beef ribs: Pull the ribs out of the refrigerator and place on a cutting board next to each other, rib bones down and pointing directly at you. On one side, place a skewer right in the center of the ribs, near where the meat and bone meet. Skewer the meat all the way through, as close to the bone as possible. Repeat on the other beef rib with the bones parallel to the first. Secure to the rotisserie using skewer prongs so the meat does not come loose on the skewer. Secure the skewers to the rotisserie.

5. Cook for about 4 hours until the internal temperature reaches 205°F (96°C), adding more coals or wood chunks, as needed, to maintain a consistent temperature so the meat cooks evenly. Also, watch for burning and flare-ups. Move the coals around or spritz with water, if necessary. Once the meat is done, pull it off the fire, cover, and let rest for 1 hour.

6. For serving, slice the meat between the bones.

BARBECUE

Ah, barbecue. This classic style of cooking has many shapes and forms throughout the world. From legendary low-and-slow styles coming out of smokers in the United States (like Tennessee, where I live) to the in-ground pit styles from Samoa, Patagonia, and more, there are so many fine examples of barbecue.

So, how do you conquer all barbecue fire cooking styles in just five recipes? Well, you don't. There are so many amazing cookbooks and recipe books out there that dive into the depths of every specific barbecue genre, but here we lightly graze the surface for what you can do with lower-heat indirect fire cooking.

So, what is barbecue? You can ask ten people and get ten different answers to this question. In this book, I define barbecue as fire cooking that utilizes the indirect method, covered with a lid or another device, while mostly cooking at lower temperatures to slowly break down food and provide a subtle smoke flavor. Join me and we will conquer some familiar styles of barbecue through recipes like Hot and Fast Bourbon Peach Ribs (page 140) and Smoked Pork Belly Burnt Ends (page 150). If you have never tired pork belly burnt ends, you are in for a treat.

Although this definition is a start, I also break out of some of the "norms" of barbecue to give you unique recipes that push the limits of fire cooking. That means venturing into baking food at higher temperatures while still getting great smoke flavor. I also cover two unique methods that add tons of flavor to your food: reverse searing and salt baking. These are not common styles of fire cooking, but after you learn about them, I think you will be converted.

Let's start with something out of the norm: Fire-Baked Lobster Tails (following). This delicious seafood delicacy is baked next to the campfire, or in your grill quickly, to get that subtle sweet smoke onto the lobster meat. It's the perfect quick recipe to inspire you to take on one of the chapter's longer cooks.

FIRE-BAKED LOBSTER TAILS

These lobster tails might not stay inside the low and slow method that other recipes adhere to, but I think they demonstrate barbecue flavor at its finest. Quickly smoked next to the fire, the lobster tails take on a subtle sweetness that pairs nicely with a simple Italian butter. You can easily cook these at the campfire, if you'd like—no grill required. Just place them in a cast-iron pan, cover with aluminum foil, and place it next to the fire.

PREP TIME: 40 MINUTES | COOK TIME: 25 MINUTES

4 servings

FOR LOBSTER TAILS

4 whole lobster tails (preferably cold water)

2 tablespoons (30 ml) olive oil

1 tablespoon (18 g) kosher salt

2 teaspoons black pepper

1 teaspoon cayenne powder

FOR ITALIAN BUTTER

½ cup (112 g) unsalted butter

1½ teaspoons chopped fresh oregano leaves

1½ teaspoons chopped fresh basil

Grated zest of 1 lemon

Juice of 1 lemon

4 garlic cloves, minced

1 teaspoon sea salt

1 teaspoon black pepper

1 teaspoon red pepper flakes

FOR SPECIAL GEAR

Enclosed grill

Cast-iron skillet

Basting brush

1. To make the lobster tails: Using a sharp knife, gently score the lobster flesh once from top to tail. Cut all the way until you get close to the end—but not all the way through. Using your hands, carefully pull the meat up and out of the shell while still leaving the end connected. Gently place the meat on top of the cut shell so it rests above the shell, being exposed. Repeat for all your lobster tails. Lather the lobster meat with oil.

2. In a small food-safe bowl, stir together the salt, black pepper, and cayenne. Season the lobster tails generously with the spices and refrigerate until ready to cook.

3. Preheat your fire using the instructions for the Barbecue method (see page 41), bringing it to a medium-high temperature (about 400°F, or 200°C).

4. Place the lobsters on the grill away from the main heat source. Cook for about 20 minutes until the meat turns from opaque to white (internal temperature of 135°F, or 57°C), adding more coals or wood, as needed, to maintain a consistent temperature.

5. To make the Italian butter: With about 5 minutes left on the cook, in a cast-iron skillet, combine all the Italian butter ingredients. Place the skillet over the heat to melt the butter and combine the flavors. Lather the outside of the lobster tails in butter sauce right before pulling them off the fire. Let rest for 2 minutes.

6. Serve the tails whole with any remaining Italian butter on the side for dipping.

HOT AND FAST
BOURBON-PEACH RIBS

Although these ribs take about 3½ hours to cook, that's about half the time traditional ribs take. Yet, you'll find they are super tender and delicious. I first fell in love with this style of cooking ribs after my friend, pitmaster Christie Vanover from GirlsCanGrill.com, showed me the method. Dang—they were out of this world! For someone who does not have the patience for a 6- to 7-hour cook on ribs, these are a great place to start. As for the bourbon peach glaze, I think that speaks for itself on the deliciousness scale.

PREP TIME: 30 MINUTES | COOK TIME: 3 HOURS 30 MINUTES

4 servings

FOR PORK RIBS

2 whole St. Louis-style pork rib slabs

2 tablespoons (22 g) yellow mustard

1½ tablespoons (27 g) kosher salt

1½ tablespoons (9 g) black pepper

1 tablespoon (7.5 g) chili powder

2 teaspoons garlic powder

2 teaspoons onion powder

FOR WRAPPING

12 tablespoons (168 g) unsalted butter, cubed

4 tablespoons (60 g) packed light brown sugar

4 tablespoons (60 g) honey

FOR BOURBON-PEACH GLAZE

2 tablespoons (30 ml) bourbon

3 tablespoons (42 g) unsalted butter

2 tablespoons (40 g) peach preserves

FOR SPECIAL GEAR

Small heatproof saucepan

1. To make the ribs: Place the ribs, bone-side up, on a work surface. Using your hands or a butter knife, lift the membrane along the bones and pull it off the ribs. Lather the pork ribs in yellow mustard.

2. In a small food-safe bowl, stir together the salt, pepper, chili powder, garlic powder, and onion powder. Season the ribs thoroughly with the spices and refrigerate to set for 15 minutes.

3. Preheat your smoker using the instructions for the Barbecue method (see page 41), bringing it to a medium temperature (about 300°F, or 150°C).

4. Place the ribs in the smoker, bone-side down. Cook for 1½ hours.

5. To make the wrapping: Tear off a piece of aluminum foil about 1½ times the length of the ribs. Spread 3 tablespoons (42 g) of cubed butter along the foil

recipe continues

with 1 tablespoon (15 g) of brown sugar and 1 tablespoon (20 g) of honey. Place the ribs, bone-side up, on the butter and distribute 3 tablespoons (42 g) of butter, 1 tablespoon (15 g) of brown sugar, and 1 tablespoon (20 g) of honey over the bones. Wrap the ribs with the foil so they are fully enclosed. Repeat with the second slab of ribs.

6. Place the wrapped ribs back into the smoker and cook for 1½ hours.

7. To make the bourbon-peach glaze: About 15 minutes before the ribs are done, place a small heatproof barbecue saucepan in the smoker. Carefully add the bourbon to the pan and cook for 5 minutes. Stir in the butter and peach preserves.

8. Once the ribs reach an internal temperature of 203°F (95°C), remove them from the foil and place them back into the smoker, bone-side down. Glaze the outside of the ribs with the bourbon-peach glaze and cook for 15 minutes until the outside is caramelized. Pull the ribs off the fire and let rest for 5 minutes.

9. For serving, cut the ribs individually or serve the whole rack.

REVERSE SEARED
SHOVEL TRI-TIP

Marinated overnight in a mustard, onion, and vinegar-based marinade for extra tenderness, this tri-tip is topped with a smoky salsa that gives it a subtle heat right at the end. But the real star of this dish is how it's cooked. Read on to learn how to use the reverse sear method on this big cut of meat to make it tender and perfectly cooked in the middle. Wait, reverse what? Reverse searing is simply the process of barbecuing a piece of meat until the internal temperature is where you want it. Then, once done, you pull it off and let it rest. Finally, you sear it off over really high heat to get a nice crust. The sear happens last, hence, reverse seared.

I first saw shovel searing by the amazing Chef Steven Raichlen a few years ago! For this recipe, I decided to break out the food-grade stainless-steel shovel. Yes, some companies do make food-grade stainless-steel shovels and they are not difficult to order online. If you don't have one and prefer not to buy one, use a cast-iron skillet or your grill grate for the sear.

PREP TIME: 30 MINUTES | MARINATING TIME: 4 HOURS | COOK TIME: 1 HOUR 30 MINUTES

4 servings

FOR GARLIC-ONION MARINADE

15 garlic cloves, peeled

1 white onion, diced

2 tablespoons (30 g) Dijon mustard

2 tablespoons (30 ml) red wine vinegar

1 tablespoon (3 g) dried oregano

1 tablespoon (7 g) ground cumin

1 tablespoon (15 ml) hot sauce

1 tablespoon (18 g) sea salt

2 teaspoons smoked paprika

2 teaspoons black pepper

FOR TRI-TIP

1 (1½- to 2-pound, or 681 to 908 g) whole tri-tip steak (preferably with fat cap attached), silverskin trimmed

1 recipe Smoked Spicy Salsa (page 181)

FOR SPECIAL GEAR

Smoker

Food-grade stainless-steel shovel or cast-iron skillet

1. To make the onion-garlic marinade: In a food processor, combine all the marinade ingredients and process thoroughly until smooth.

2. To make the tri-tip: Trim any remaining silverskin and any excess fat—leaving the fat cap on—from the tri-tip. Score the fat cap in a crosshatch pattern in ½-inch (1 cm) segments. Place the tri-tip into a large food-safe bowl and pour in the marinade. Cover and refrigerate to marinate for at least 4 hours or, ideally, overnight. About halfway through the marinating time, flip the tri-tip for an even marinade.

recipe continues

3. Preheat your smoker using the instructions for the Barbecue method (see page 41), bringing it to a low temperature (about 225°F, or 107°C).

4. Remove the tri-tip from the marinade and place it in the smoker. Cook for 1 to 1½ hours until the internal temperature reaches 120°F (49°C). Pull the meat off the fire and let rest for 15 minutes.

5. As your tri-tip rests, preheat your fire using the instruction for Grilling (see page 29), bringing it to a high temperature (about 450°F, or 230°C). Place a food-grade stainless-steel shovel into the fire to preheat for about 5 minutes. If you do not have a shovel, place a cast-iron skillet or the grill grate.

6. Place tri-tip on the shovel, fat-side down, and sear for about 1 minute. Carefully flip the tri-tip and sear the other side for about 1 minute. Once nicely seared on all sides, pull the steak off the fire and let rest for 2 minutes.

7. To slice the tri-tip, position the steak on a cutting board facing like an "L." Make your first slice at a 45-degree angle, cutting the "L" in half. Rotate one side 90 degrees so you are now slicing the meat against the grain. Slice the tri-tip into thin pieces from both halves of the steak.

8. For serving, top with the smoked spicy salsa.

SALT-BAKED RED SNAPPER

The premise of salt baking is that you trap the food's moisture inside a salt crust to cook it without drying out the food. There are no big secrets. Just read the instructions that follow thoroughly regarding the water to salt ratio to create the ideal salt crust.

PREP TIME: 1 HOUR | COOK TIME: 1 HOUR

2 servings

FOR SEASONING

1 tablespoon (18 g) kosher salt

1 tablespoon (6 g) black pepper

2 teaspoons ground cumin

1 teaspoon cayenne powder

Grated zest of 1 lemon

Grated zest of 1 lime

Juice of 1 lemon

Juice of 1 lime

2 tablespoons (30 ml) olive oil

FOR RED SNAPPER

1 whole red snapper, gutted and cleaned

1 lemon, sliced

1 lime, sliced

6 cilantro sprigs

6 parsley sprigs

FOR SALT CRUST

7½ pounds (3.4 kg) kosher salt, plus more as needed

1 cup (240 ml) water, plus more as needed

6 lemons, sliced

6 limes, sliced

1. To make the seasoning: In a small food-safe bowl, stir together the salt, black pepper, cumin, cayenne, lemon and lime zest, lemon and lime juice, and oil until a paste forms.

2. To make the red snapper: Start by removing the fins from the snapper and scoring the skin with 3 cuts down the fish only ¼ inch (0.6 cm) deep.

3. Lather the red snapper, inside and out, with the seasoning paste. Stuff the snapper with the lemon and lime slices and cilantro and parsley sprigs.

4. Pull out a large sheet pan, about 1½ times the size of your fish.

5. To make the salt crust: In a large bowl, stir together the salt and water until you have a sand-like texture. Spread half the salt mixture on the sheet pan. Using about half the fruit, top with a layer of lemon and lime slices in an area big enough to accommodate the fish. Place the fish on the citrus slices. Top the fish with the remaining lemon and lime slices, then cover the fish entirely with the remaining salt until the only parts of the fish exposed are the head and the end of the tail. Mix together more salt and water, as needed, in a ratio of 1 ounce (30 ml) of water for every 12 ounces (340 g) of salt. Carefully place the fish into the refrigerator until ready to cook.

6. Preheat your smoker using the instructions for the Barbecue method (see page 41), bringing it to a high temperature (about 400°F, or 200°C).

recipe continues

7. Carefully place the sheet pan with the red snapper into the smoker. Cook for 45 minutes to 1 hour, or until the internal temperature reaches about 145°F (63°C). The outside salt crust should begin to harden as the fish cooks to a point that it becomes thick. Carefully press a probe into the fish, careful not to break the crust, when checking the temperature. Pull the fish off the fire and let rest for 5 minutes.

8. For serving, carefully peel off the salt crust and brush off any excess salt left on the fish. Serve the fish whole.

What Is Salt Baking?

Using salt is one way to retain moisture in food; the point of salt baking is to encapsulate your food in a thick layer of salt so the moisture stays inside the meat and cannot escape. We start by mixing salt with water to create an almost sand-like consistency. For those who want to be even more fancy, add egg whites to the mixture for a firmer crust, about 4 whites for every 1 pound (454 g) of salt; you can replace the water with egg whites, too. We then cover the entire cut of meat in a salt crust. Do not worry; the crust will not make the food overly salty, as the crust pulls away from the food in large chunks when finished. If you are worried about saltiness, place a layer of parchment paper between the meat and the salt crust. Cook the food until it is done, then pull off the salt to reveal a perfectly cooked piece of meat. This is a fun way to cook whole fish, beef tenderloin, even leg of lamb.

SMOKED PORK BELLY BURNT ENDS

Pork belly is simply uncured, unsmoked, and unsliced bacon. I originally fell in love with pork belly burnt ends at a barbecue festival in rural Tennessee—covered in a whiskey barbecue sauce that was absolutely insane. I had to make some the following week! Eventually, I ended using my maple-bourbon glaze because it packs an amazing flavor with the caramel sweetness of the bourbon and the classic sweetness of the maple syrup. It's the key to these sweet caramelized nuggets. Make these at your next barbecue or for a holiday dinner and watch them disappear.

PREP TIME: 35 MINUTES | COOK TIME: 4 HOURS

10 servings

FOR SEASONING

1½ tablespoons (27 g) kosher salt

1½ tablespoons (9 g) black pepper

1 tablespoon (8.4 g) smoked paprika

1 tablespoon (15 g) light brown sugar

1½ teaspoons garlic powder

1½ teaspoons onion powder

FOR PORK BELLY

2 pounds (908 g) pork belly

2 tablespoons (30 ml) olive oil

6 tablespoons (84 g) unsalted butter, cubed

½ cup (120 g) packed light brown sugar

1 recipe Maple-Bourbon Glaze (page 196), warmed

FOR SPECIAL GEAR

Smoker

Basting brush

1. To make the seasoning: In a small food-safe bowl, stir together all the seasoning ingredients. Set aside.

2. To make the pork belly: Start by cubing the pork belly into 1-inch (2.5 cm) pieces. Place all the pork belly cubes into a large bowl and lather with oil. Thoroughly season the pork belly with the spices. Refrigerate to set for 2 hours.

3. Preheat your smoker using the instructions for the Barbecue method (see page 41), bringing it to a low temperature (about 250°F, or 120°C). Line a sheet pan with aluminum foil and set aside.

4. Place the pork belly directly onto the smoker and cook for 2½ hours, adding more wood and charcoal, as needed, to maintain a consistent temperature. Once the pork belly is tender and auburn-brown, pull it off the fire and transfer to the prepared sheet pan. Top the pork belly with the cubed butter and brown sugar. Cover the pork with an aluminum foil sheet and return to the smoker for 1½ hours.

5. When the pork is close to done, pour the maple-bourbon glaze over the top and mix everything thoroughly. Increase the temperature of the smoker to medium-high heat (375°F, or 190°C). Let the pork belly caramelize for 5 to 10 minutes until it reaches an internal temperature of 205°F (96°C). Your temperature probe should easily slide into the pork belly with no resistance when it is done. Pull the pork belly off the fire and let rest for about 5 minutes. Serve the pork belly directly out of the foil-lined pan.

4

VEGETABLES AND SIDES

As a kid, I hated vegetables. I never wanted to eat Brussels sprouts, broccoli, or spinach when I could be eating grilled steak or rotisserie chicken! While I am still no herbivore, I am something of an advocate for vegetables grilled over fire. In fact, whenever I am taken to a fancy steakhouse or a fire-cooked dinner, it is often not the meat I try first but the sides. They can be a true test of a great chef as they take deliberate effort to make them extraordinarily delicious. I believe anyone can cook a great-tasting steak but finding a way to make veggies shine is a whole other level.

That is what we will conquer in this section: elevating vegetables and sides. Not all are wrapped in bacon and covered in sugar, but I can't resist sharing my Grilled Bacon-Wrapped Asparagus (page 159). Perhaps the Grilled Artichokes (page 156) and the Charred Brussels Sprouts (page 155) are better examples of how fire can do the heavy lifting. It is one of my favorite dishes in this whole book to cook—the Brussels sprouts are lightly charred until crispy. The result is far from the vegetable I feared as a kid.

As for starches, I cover some fun ways to cook potatoes, from Grilled Potato Wedges (page 170) to Smashed Potatoes with Chipotle-Garlic Mayo. (No, that is not a typo. I mean smashed.) These awesome potatoes are parboiled until soft, smashed, and grilled over fire like a flat patty . . . amazing flavor (page 174)!

I even show you how to make Coal-Roasted Flatbread with Parmesan and Rosemary (page 163). Cooked right on the coals, this is an epic appetizer for those who want to amaze guests and friends. So, get ready to take sides to a whole new level.

CHARRED BRUSSELS SPROUTS

There is, perhaps, no other vegetable that can be as disappointing—or as amazing—as Brussels sprouts, depending on how you cook them. Done poorly, they can be watery and unappetizing. But by cooking them over the fire, they become crispy perfection. In this recipe, the charred outside takes on a nice tang from a hit of vinegar while the inside of the Brussels sprouts remains tender. When I'm in the mood for something a little different, I swap out the vinegar for lemon juice and top these with Parmesan cheese, similar to the treatment I give the Grilled Bacon-Wrapped Asparagus (page 159).

PREP TIME: 15 MINUTES | COOK TIME: 15 MINUTES

4 servings

2 tablespoons (30 ml) canola oil

1 pound Brussels sprouts, halved

1½ tablespoons (23 ml) red wine vinegar

2 teaspoons sea salt

2 teaspoons black pepper

1 teaspoon red pepper flakes

FOR SPECIAL GEAR

Cast-iron skillet

1. Preheat your fire using the instructions for the Skillet method (see page 30), bringing it to a medium-high temperature (about 375°F, or 190°C).

2. Place the oil in a cast-iron skillet and place the skillet over the coals for 2 minutes before cooking.

3. Carefully add the Brussels sprouts to the skillet, cut-side down. Cook for about 5 minutes, then stir.

4. Stir in the vinegar, salt, black pepper, and red pepper flakes until the sprouts are well coated. Continue cooking the Brussels sprouts for 7 to 8 minutes, or until crispy, charred, and bright green. You're ready to serve.

GRILLED ARTICHOKES

While out in California cooking for an event, I was introduced to this dish by Chef Frank Ostini, of the Hitching Post II. While I have enjoyed artichokes my whole life, I had never tasted them grilled over the fire until that day. The essence of smoke and char the artichokes took on while being cooked over a direct flame was astounding. It was like having a whole new vegetable I had never eaten! This is my take on Frank's inspiring dish—a starter that just might steal the show from the meat.

PREP TIME: 30 MINUTES | COOK TIME: 35 MINUTES

4 servings

FOR ARTICHOKES

2 teaspoons sea salt, plus a pinch

4 large artichokes, halved with stem

2 teaspoons black pepper

1 teaspoon garlic powder

1 tablespoon (15 ml) olive oil

FOR DIPPING SAUCE

¼ cup (60 g) yogurt

2 tablespoons (30 g) mayonnaise

4 garlic cloves, pressed

2 tablespoons (2 g) finely chopped fresh cilantro

Juice of 1 lemon

Grated zest of 1 lemon

1. To make the artichokes: Preheat your fire using the instructions for the Skillet method (see page 30), bringing it to a high temperature (about 400°F, or 200°C).

2. Fill a large stainless-steel stockpot or soup pot with enough water to cover the artichokes by at least 2 inches (5 cm). Add a pinch of salt and place the pot over the fire. Bring the water to a roaring boil.

3. Add the artichokes to the pot. Cook, uncovered, for about 7 minutes. Flip the artichokes, so they cook evenly, and cook for about 8 minutes more until they become softened on the outside, which also indicates the middle core is done. Drain, pat dry with paper towel, and set aside.

4. In a small bowl, stir together the salt, pepper, and garlic powder. Lather the artichoke halves with oil and season the inside (cut-side) with the salt mix. Set aside.

5. Preheat your fire using the instructions for Grilling (see page 29), bringing it to a medium-high temperature (about 375°F, or 190°C).

6. Place the artichokes on the grill. Cook for 8 to 10 minutes until they are well charred. Pull the artichokes off the fire and set aside.

7. To make the dipping sauce: In a medium-size bowl, stir together the sauce ingredients until well blended.

8. Place the artichokes, cut-side up, on a plate and serve the dipping sauce on the side.

GRILLED BACON-WRAPPED ASPARAGUS

If you have never had bacon-wrapped asparagus, you have not lived! No, seriously. This recipe takes those two great ingredients and layers on more flavor with lemon and Parmesan. Being wrapped in bacon, this dish was quickly added to our family fire-cooking dinners. Use asparagus on the thicker side so it holds up well once the bacon is wrapped around it and so you have room to skewer it. Also, watch for flare-ups to avoid burnt bacon. It is easy to burn bacon over an open flame, so keep a close eye.

PREP TIME: 20 MINUTES | COOK TIME: 15 MINUTES

4 servings

1 bunch (12 or 16 spears) large asparagus, woody ends trimmed

8 ounces thin-sliced cured bacon

3 tablespoons (42 g) unsalted butter, melted

2 tablespoons (12.5 g) grated Parmesan cheese

2 teaspoons fresh lemon juice

1 teaspoon grated lemon zest

½ teaspoon red pepper flakes

FOR SPECIAL EQUIPMENT

Basting brush

1. Arrange the asparagus into groups of 3 or 4 spears similar in size. Carefully wrap 1 bacon slice around the center of each asparagus bundle, skewering a toothpick at an angle through the loose end of the bacon and through the bundle so the toothpick emerges on the other side. Make sure your toothpick secures the bacon to the bundle, then set aside.

2. Preheat your fire using the instructions for Grilling (see page 29), bringing it to a medium-high temperature (about 375°F, or 190°C). Thoroughly clean your grill grate before cooking.

3. Once the coals are ready, place the asparagus bundles on the grill. Cook for about 12 minutes, rotating to all sides every 2 to 3 minutes to crisp the bacon all over. Move the bacon-wrapped asparagus away from the flame if it begins to flare. Once the bacon is crispy and the asparagus is soft, pull it off the fire and let rest for 2 minutes to cool.

4. In a small bowl, stir together the melted butter, Parmesan, lemon juice, lemon zest, and red pepper flakes. Using a basting brush, glaze the top of the bacon-wrapped asparagus with the butter sauce, or serve the sauce on the side for dipping.

SEARED TOMATO AND ARUGULA

Sometimes you just want something fresh . . . but that doesn't mean you can't char it over the fire. In this recipe, charred tomatoes are paired with fresh arugula, toasted almonds, red onion, mozzarella, and a hit of balsamic. It's a classic flavor combination for a reason, but I think you'll find the character of the tomatoes takes the dish to another level. Use pine nuts instead of almonds, if you want, and feel free to drizzle some olive oil on top to make it more savory.

PREP TIME: 15 MINUTES | COOK TIME: 15 MINUTES

4 servings

2 tablespoons (11.5 g) sliced almonds

2½ tablespoons (38 ml) canola oil

1 cup (149 g) cherry tomatoes, halved

1½ cups (30 g) fresh arugula

2 tablespoons (20 g) thinly sliced red onion

Juice of 1 lemon

1 (8-ounce, or 225 g) ball fresh mozzarella, cut into slices

2½ tablespoons (38 ml) balsamic vinaigrette

FOR SPECIAL GEAR

Cast-iron skillet

1. Preheat your fire using the instructions for the Skillet method (see page 30), bringing it to a medium-high temperature (about 375°F, or 190°C).

2. Preheat a cast-iron skillet over the coals for 2 minutes before cooking.

3. Place the almonds into the skillet. Let them roast for about 2 minutes, stirring frequently, until they are slightly toasted. Remove the almonds from the skillet and set aside.

4. Pour the oil into your skillet. Add the cherry tomatoes, cut-side down. Cook the tomatoes for 3 to 4 minutes until they begin to char and caramelize. Once blackened, pull them out of the skillet and set aside.

5. In a medium-size bowl, toss the arugula and red onion to combine. Squeeze the lemon juice on top and toss to coat evenly. Top the arugula with the charred tomatoes, mozzarella slices, and toasted almonds. Drizzle the vinaigrette on top and enjoy.

COAL-ROASTED FLATBREAD WITH PARMESAN AND ROSEMARY

The first time I saw someone make coal-roasted bread, I was mesmerized. It was so fast and quick—I had no idea it could be done so easily over the fire. I recommend trying this recipe with your favorite prepared pizza dough, but you can use most flatbread-style doughs. Whatever dough you use, you will need to be able to roll it out easily as you want a relatively thin oval shape to get the result pictured here.

As long as you get those coals super-hot (see Cooking on the Coal, page 33), all you need do is lay the bread on them and let the fire do the rest. If your fire is hot enough, the bread will crust up really fast—like a steak—and be ready to flip in just 1 to 2 minutes. Top this guy off with the Parmesan-rosemary spread, or get crazy with fresh herbs, spices, cheese—even fruit!

PREP TIME: 20 MINUTES | CHILLING TIME: 30 MINUTES | COOK TIME: 5 MINUTES

4 servings

All-purpose flour, for working the dough

1 pound (454 g) raw pizza dough

1 tablespoon (1.7 g) fresh rosemary leaves

5 garlic cloves, minced

1 tablespoon (6.25 g) grated Parmesan cheese

¼ cup (60 ml) olive oil

1. Spread a handful of flour on a flat surface and place the dough on it. Add some flour to your hands and carefully knead the pizza dough. Begin to flatten the dough into an oval shape, no more than 1 inch (2.5 cm) thick. Continue to add flour, as needed. Place the flat dough in the refrigerator for 30 minutes to firm.

2. Preheat your fire using the instructions for the Coal method (see page 33). Once your coals are white-hot, blow off any ash on top.

3. While the dough chills, in a small bowl, stir together the rosemary, garlic, Parmesan, and oil. Set aside.

4. A few minutes before you are ready to cook, pull the dough out of the refrigerator and let it come to room temperature.

5. Once the coals are glowing red, place the dough on the coals. Cook for 1 to 2 minutes, or until the edges turn brown and begin to char. Carefully flip the bread, brushing off any coals and place it back down on the hot coals. Cook for 1 to 2 minutes until charred on all sides, crispy, and firm. Pull it off the fire and let rest for 2 minutes.

6. Glaze the top of the bread with the Parmesan-rosemary spread and any other toppings you choose.

Variations on a Flatbread

Cooking flatbread on the coals was one of the first things I learned to do on my fire-cooking journey. Although I have perfected my method, there are tons of variations you can make for coal-roasted flatbreads. From savory to sweet, here are three fun ideas:

Barbecue Chicken Ranch: This fun twist is less formal than other flatbreads. I love heating leftover shredded chicken in a skillet next to my flatbread. Right before pulling the bread off, lather it with a thin layer of your favorite barbecue sauce and some shredded mozzarella cheese. Let that melt for just a few seconds until it is nice and gooey. Pull it off the coals and top it with the chicken and some sliced red onion. Add a drizzle of ranch dressing and you are ready to go!

Goat Cheese and Prosciutto: For those who really want to impress, this flatbread will do the job. Cook the flatbread (see Coal-Roasted Flatbread with Parmesan and Rosemary, page 163), and pull it off the coals when done. Top with a layer of prosciutto and place a few dollops of goat cheese on top. For added fun, add sliced dates and a drizzle of honey for some sweetness. This is a great appetizer before grilling the main meal over fire.

Hazelnut and Fruit: One of my favorite ways to serve coal-roasted flatbread is for dessert. Although that might seem crazy, I assure you it is out-of-this-world delicious. Cook the flatbread (see Coal-Roasted Flatbread with Parmesan and Rosemary, page 163), and pull it off the coals when done. Smear a thin layer of hazelnut spread on top along with an assortment of fresh fruit. We love strawberries, blueberries, and raspberries but use what you can get locally.

COWBOY-BROILED CHEESY BROCCOLI

One of the few things I have found hard to do when cooking with live fire is broiling, similar to how you would broil in an oven. To broil is to cook from the top down at high heat to sear off, cook, or caramelize a crust. I thought it was all but impossible until I discovered the cowboy broil. I do not remember who showed me this technique, but the idea is to cover your skillet with aluminum foil, then place charcoal on top to replicate the top-down broil. This Cowboy-Broiled Cheesy Broccoli is the perfect dish to try this technique. Once you get the hang of it, try it with steaks, eggs with cheese, and tons more.

PREP TIME: 15 MINUTES | COOK TIME: 10 MINUTES

4 servings

2 cups (142 g) broccoli florets, washed

6 garlic cloves, minced

2 teaspoons kosher salt

2 teaspoons black pepper

2 tablespoons (30 ml) canola oil

2 tablespoons (28 g) unsalted butter

1 cup (115 g) shredded sharp Cheddar cheese

2 tablespoons (14 g) bread crumbs

FOR SPECIAL GEAR

Cast-iron skillet

1. In a large food-safe bowl, stir together the broccoli, garlic, salt, pepper, and oil. Set aside.

2. Preheat your fire using the instructions for the Skillet method (see page 30), bringing it to a medium-high temperature (about 375°F, or 190°).

3. Place the butter in a cast-iron skillet and place the skillet over the coals for 2 minutes before cooking.

4. Add the broccoli to the skillet. Cook for about 8 minutes until the broccoli is soft, bright green, and slightly charred. When done, pull the broccoli off the heat.

5. Top the broccoli with the Cheddar cheese, carefully cover the skillet with aluminum foil, and top the foil with enough hot coals from the fire to cover the foil (about three-fourths of the skillet should be covered). Cook the broccoli for 2 minutes, adding more coals, as needed, to "broil" all parts of the skillet. Remove the foil and let cool for 2 minutes. The dish will be cheesy, bubbly, and nicely caramelized. Top with bread crumbs before serving.

CARAMELIZED CARROTS

Some meats just scream for a side that's rich and sweet. These caramelized carrots are no health food—they are sweet and rich thanks to a brown sugar and butter sauce. Cooked in cast iron so you do not lose any of that precious sauce to the coals, these carrots also bring plenty of texture to the plate. They cook up tender but also have crispy bits . . . you just may find them gone before you expected and need to make a second batch! I like to pair these carrots with the Herb Brush-Basted Bone-In Rib Eye (page 49), Rotisserie Leg of Lamb (page 130), or smoked pork ribs.

PREP TIME: 15 MINUTES | COOK TIME: 15 MINUTES

4 servings

3 tablespoons (42 g) unsalted butter, melted

1 tablespoon (15 g) light brown sugar

2 teaspoons kosher salt

1½ tablespoons (23 ml) canola oil

1 pound (454 g) whole carrots, topped and cleaned

FOR SPECIAL GEAR

Cast-iron skillet

Basting brush

1. In a small food-safe bowl, stir together the melted butter, brown sugar, and salt. Set aside.

2. Preheat your fire using the instructions for the Skillet method (see page 30), bringing it to a medium-high temperature (about 375°F, or 190°C).

3. Place the oil in a cast-iron skillet and place the skillet over the coals for 2 minutes before cooking.

4. Add the carrots to the skillet. Cook for about 10 minutes until they begin to brown.

5. Using a basting brush, glaze the carrots with the butter mixture. Continue to cook for 5 to 7 minutes, rotating and basting every 1 to 2 minutes, until the carrots are soft and caramelized on the outside. Pull the carrots off the fire and let cool for 1 minute.

6. Glaze the outside of the carrots with the remaining butter sauce and serve.

GRILLED POTATO WEDGES

This is an awesome side to make with Skirt Steak with Spicy Cilantro Chimichurri (page 39), Brazilian-Inspired Picanha (page 126), or Hanging Chicken (page 104), as these take a while to cook. If the potato wedges are done early, set them to the cooler side of the grill to keep warm while you finish the rest of the cook. These wedges are all about the delicious crispiness they take on cooked right over the fire. If you want a dipping sauce, try Classic Chimichurri (page 179), Spicy Cilantro Chimichurri (page 180), or Creamy Horseradish Sauce (page 85).

PREP TIME: 25 MINUTES | COOK TIME: 20 MINUTES

4 servings

4 russet potatoes, washed

2 tablespoons (30 ml) canola oil

2 teaspoons kosher salt

2 teaspoons garlic powder

1 teaspoon black pepper

1 teaspoon red pepper flakes

1. On a cutting board, carefully cut the potatoes into wedges. Start by halving them lengthwise. Then, lay one half flat on the board. Slicing at an angle, cut the potato half into wedges, ¾ to 1 inch (2–2.5 cm) thick. Cut all potatoes and place the wedges in a large food-safe bowl. Add the oil, salt, garlic powder, black pepper, and red pepper flakes. Toss to coat evenly. Set aside.

2. Preheat your fire using the instructions for Grilling (see page 29), bringing it to a medium-high temperature (about 375°F, or 190°C).

3. Place the potatoes on the grill. Cook for 5 to 7 minutes per side until they are golden brown on the outside. The potatoes are done once you can press a toothpick into them with little resistance. Pull the potatoes off the fire and let rest for 2 minutes.

SMOKED SWEET POTATOES

Sweet potatoes are a little slice of dessert for dinner that doesn't make you feel guilty. So, if you are looking for something to sweeten up the holidays or a classic backyard cookout, look no further. Pair these with any recipes from the Barbecue section of the book (see page 136), like the Hot and Fast Bourbon Peach Ribs (page 140), and you will be in hog heaven. The subtle smoke flavor paired with the natural sweetness of sweet potatoes makes a great base to drizzle some brown sugar butter over.

PREP TIME: 15 MINUTES | COOK TIME: 2 HOURS

4 servings

4 sweet potatoes, cleaned

2 tablespoons (30 g) light brown sugar

2 teaspoons ground cinnamon

2 teaspoons kosher salt

1 teaspoon allspice

4 tablespoons (56 g) unsalted butter

1 tablespoon (20 g) honey

1. Using a fork, poke a few holes in the skin of the sweet potatoes. Set them aside.

2. Preheat your fire using the instructions for Barbecue (see page 41), bringing it to a medium-low temperature (about 275°F, or 140°C).

3. Place the sweet potatoes into the smoker and cook for about 1 hour, or until they begin to soften inside. Wrap the sweet potatoes in aluminum foil and return to the smoker for 1 hour until completely softened. Pull the sweet potatoes off the and let cool for 2 minutes.

4. While the sweet potatoes cook, in a small bowl, stir together the brown sugar, cinnamon, salt, and allspice. Set aside.

5. Slit open the cooked sweet potatoes. Top each with 1 tablespoon (14 g) of butter, a sprinkle of spices, and a drizzle of honey. Serve immediately.

SMASHED POTATOES WITH CHIPOTLE-GARLIC MAYO

We all love mashed potatoes and baked potatoes, but smashed potatoes just might be the best preparation of all. You start by parboiling golden potatoes, cooked until they are almost done but not too soft. Then, smash them into patties to grill over the fire. They are excellent paired with Salt-Pepper-Cinnamon Rib Eye with Butter Baste (page 68), Skirt Steak with Chimichurri (page 59), Hanging Chicken (page 104), and even eggs. Use medium-size golden potatoes, as they are the best size and flavor for this preparation. If you want them extra crispy, finish them by pan-frying in hot oil.

PREP TIME: 15 MINUTES | COOK TIME: 35 MINUTES

4 servings

FOR CHIPOTLE-GARLIC MAYO

2 tablespoons (30 g) mayonnaise

2 tablespoons (34 g) chipotle peppers in adobo sauce, puréed

2 garlic cloves, pressed

Juice of 1 lime

FOR POTATOES

1 tablespoon (18 g) kosher salt, plus a pinch

8 medium-size golden potatoes, washed

2 tablespoons (30 ml) olive oil

2 teaspoons black pepper

2 teaspoons granulated garlic

1 teaspoon ground cumin

1 teaspoon dried oregano

1 teaspoon dried parsley

½ teaspoon dried thyme

FOR SPECIAL GEAR

8-quart stainless-steel pot

Basting brush

1. To make the chipotle-garlic mayo: In a small bowl, stir together the mayo, chipotle, garlic, and lime juice. Cover and refrigerate until needed.

2. To make the potatoes: Preheat your fire using the instructions for the Skillet method (see page 30), bringing it to a high temperature (about 400°F, or 200°C).

3. Fill a stainless-steel pot with enough water to cover the potatoes by at least 2 inches (5 cm). Add a pinch of salt and place it over the coals. Bring the water to a roaring boil.

4. Add the potatoes to the water and cook for 8 to 9 minutes until softened but not cooked all the way through. Pull the pot off the fire and drain the potatoes.

5. Place the potatoes on a hard surface. Using your hand or a hard surface (skillet or cutting board), firmly press down on the potatoes until they are mostly flattened—don't press too hard, though; we want them flat but intact. Using a basting brush, brush the potatoes with oil and set aside.

6. In a small bowl, stir together the salt, pepper, garlic, cumin, oregano, parsley. and thyme until thoroughly combined, then sprinkle over the potatoes.

7. Preheat your fire using the instructions for Grilling (see page 29), bringing it to a medium-high temperature (about 375°F, or 190°C).

8. Place the potatoes on the grill. Cook for 4 to 5 minutes per side until the patties are crispy golden. Pull the potatoes off the fire and let cool for 2 to 3 minutes.

9. Top each smashed potato with a dollop of chipotle-garlic mayo and serve.

5
SAUCES, MARINADES, AND RUBS

I have found that the unsung hero of many a delicious meal is the sauce, marinade, or rub. True, it is important to get that perfect medium-rare on the steak, or the right cook to enjoy those fall-off-the-bone smoked ribs. However, it can be the marinating process done before a protein hits the grill, the seasoned proportions mixed before it is seared off, or the finishing glaze that makes the difference. Welcome to my world of sauces, marinades, and rubs for fire cooking.

I love sauces, marinades, and rubs so much that I have a whole line of spices on the market for you to try (shameless plug). And although at busier times it is nice—even essential!—to buy premade seasonings, sauces, and marinades, you can get lots of satisfaction from making them at home. There are also some recipes you just have to make fresh, like Classic Chimichurri (page 179). This South American staple has been a mainstay in my family for more than 4 years. With only a few ingredients, you have one of the best sauces money can buy. I use it as a dipping sauce for skirt steak or a marinade for chicken. It is highly functional and super useful. That is the whole point.

In fact, I include here only recipes for sauces, marinades, and rubs that can be used in multiple ways. Try my Charred Salsa Verde (page 182) as a perfect starter with chips, a topping for grilled steak, or a marinade for breakfast skirt steak tacos. Add some flavor to your pork ribs or shoulders with my Maple-Bourbon Glaze (page 196). This simple yet delicious glaze can also be used on chicken (see Bacon-Wrapped Maple-Bourbon Chicken Skewers, page 123).

True workhorses, my Simple Barbecue Seasoning (page 194) and Chipotle Rub (page 191) can be added to hanging pineapple (see Charred and Glazed Pineapple, page), grilled chicken, or charred carrots. You can even mix these seasonings with some oil to create a wet paste, making it easy to lather large cuts of meat. Think creatively with these sauces, marinades, and rubs because they are so delicious you will want to use them every way you can.

CLASSIC CHIMICHURRI

I love trying recipes and sauces that are out of the norm when grilling. However, it is hard to beat a classic chimichurri. From the fresh herbal flavor of the parsley and oregano to the sharp tanginess of the red wine vinegar, chimichurri is the ideal pairing with fatty chunks of meat because it cuts through the fat, delivering a refreshing hit of flavor and acidity. Try this recipe with skirt steak, beef rib, leg of lamb, or even as a marinade.

PREP TIME: 10 MINUTES

1 cup (240 ml); 8 servings

¼ cup (60 ml) olive oil

¼ cup (16 g) chopped fresh parsley

2 tablespoons (8 g) chopped fresh oregano

2 tablespoons (30 ml) red wine vinegar

1 tablespoon (10 g) minced garlic

1 teaspoon sea salt

1 teaspoon black pepper

1 teaspoon red pepper flakes

1. In a medium-size bowl, stir together all ingredients thoroughly. Refrigerate any leftover sauce in an airtight container for up to 3 days.

What Is Chimichurri?

Hailing from South America, chimichurri is the pride of Argentinian cuisine. This herbal sauce is most often made with fresh parsley, garlic, fresh oregano, red pepper flakes, olive oil, and red wine vinegar. It is absolutely delicious paired with hearty meats, as the bright flavors of the herbs and vinegar help cut through the fat. In my house, we use it as a sauce for topping cooked meat as well as a marinade. Try chimichurri-marinated chicken wings or pork chops as a fun twist with tons of flavor. The recipe can also be adapted to make quasi-chimichurri sauces. My Spicy Cilantro Chimichurri (page 180) utilizes the same framework for traditional chimichurri, but with nontraditional ingredients. Overall, chimichurri is an essential sauce to the fire-cooking community—not only for its delicious flavor but also for its deep ties to South American fire-cooking tradition.

SPICY CILANTRO CHIMICHURRI

Chimichurri is one of the first sauces I fell in love with, so in addition to a classic recipe (see page 179), I wanted to share a variation that breaks out of the traditional mold. Having spent a period of my life in West Texas, I have always been inspired by the flavors of the Southwest. This spicy cilantro chimichurri is exactly that: an ode to South America and the Southwest. With the traditional parsley and red wine vinegar, this chimichurri keeps to its roots. Yet, it features a few twists—like serrano peppers, jalapeños, and cilantro. It is a great complement to any meat cooked over fire. In fact, double the proportions for an amazing marinade.

PREP TIME: 15 MINUTES

1½ cups (360 ml); 12 servings

¼ cup (60 ml) olive oil

¼ cup (16 g) chopped fresh parsley

2 tablespoons (2 g) chopped fresh cilantro

2 tablespoons (30 ml) red wine vinegar

1 tablespoon (6 g) chopped scallion, green parts only

1 tablespoon (10 g) minced garlic

1½ teaspoons chopped serrano pepper

1½ teaspoons chopped jalapeño pepper

1 teaspoon sea salt

1 teaspoon black pepper

1 teaspoon red pepper flakes

1. In a medium-size bowl, stir together all ingredients thoroughly. Refrigerate any leftover sauce in an airtight container for up to 3 days.

SMOKED SPICY SALSA

This smoked spicy salsa is exactly what it sounds like—smoked veggies are the star. This is the kind of salsa that fills a room with an enticing aroma, making everyone hungry. It is the perfect dish to serve with chips or veggies as a starter. Plus, it is a fresh and delicious topping on grilled meats. Try it on tri-tip, rib eye, whole chicken, pork loin, or grilled fish. Whatever is left over can be serve on the side for dipping.

PREP TIME: 15 MINUTES | COOK TIME: 1 HOUR

*1 cup (260 ml);
8 servings*

2 Roma tomatoes, cut into wedges

1 jalapeño pepper

½ white onion

5 garlic cloves, peeled

2 tablespoons (2 g) chopped fresh cilantro

1 tablespoon (17 g) chipotle peppers in adobo sauce

2 teaspoons kosher salt

Juice of 2 limes

FOR SPECIAL GEAR

Smoker

1. Preheat your smoker using the instructions for the Barbecue method (see page 41), bringing it to a low temperature (about 225°F, or 107°C).

2. Place the tomatoes, jalapeño, and onion into the smoker. Place the garlic cloves in a cast-iron skillet or aluminum foil bowl for more stability and into the smoker. Smoke the veggies for 1 hour until smoked on the outside, with a slight brown hue. Pull them out of the smoker and set aside to cool. Transfer to a food processor.

3. Add the remaining salsa ingredients to the food processor. Blend until smooth. Transfer to an airtight container and refrigerate for up to 3 days.

Pictured on page 183, bottom.

CHARRED SALSA VERDE

This charred salsa verde demonstrates how flavor from the fire can be pulled into the sauce. You start by roasting the veggies on the coals to cook them and caramelize their outside shells. This infuses aroma and flavor right into the salsa. This is an excellent topping for tacos, dipping sauce for steak, or use it to smother eggs. Want to push the boundaries? Try this as a marinade on flank steak.

PREP TIME: 15 MINUTES | COOK TIME: 10 MINUTES

1 cup (240 ml);
8 servings

3 tomatillos, husked

1 jalapeño pepper

½ white onion, diced

4 garlic cloves, peeled

¼ cup (4 g) fresh cilantro

1 (4-ounce, or 115 g) can green chilies

1 tablespoon (18 g) sea salt

Juice of 2 limes

FOR SPECIAL GEAR:

Cast-iron skillet

1. Preheat your fire using the instructions for the Skillet method (see page 30), bringing it to a medium-high temperature (about 375°F, or 190°).

2. Preheat a cast-iron skillet over the coals 2 minutes before cooking.

3. In the skillet, combine the tomatillos, jalapeno, onion, and garlic. Let them char in the skillet for 3 to 5 minutes. Look for blistering all around the edges until they are mostly covered in char. The onion should char as well and become slightly translucent. Pull the skillet off the fire and let rest for 2 minutes.

4. Transfer the blistered veggies to a blender and add the remaining ingredients. Blend until smooth with a nice salsa-like texture. Pour the sauce into an airtight container and refrigerate for up to 3 days.

Pictured on page 183, top.

CREAMY HORSERADISH SAUCE

For my wife, there is nothing better than a smoked Hanging Prime Rib (page 112) with a side of Creamy Horseradish Sauce. Not only is this an awesome companion for beef, but it crushes it with grilled chicken or pork. My take on this sauce is pretty balanced; if you need more heat, don't be afraid to up the prepared horseradish or hot sauce. That should do the trick.

PREP TIME: 10 MINUTES

Makes ½ cup (about 115 g); 4 servings

2½ tablespoons (35 g) sour cream

1 tablespoon (14 g) mayonnaise

2 tablespoons (30 g) prepared horseradish

1½ tablespoons (23 ml) hot sauce

1 tablespoon (15 g) Dijon mustard

4 garlic cloves, minced

1 teaspoon sea salt

1. In a small food-safe bowl, stir together all the sauce ingredients until well blended. Refrigerate in an airtight container for up to 3 days.

STEAKHOUSE HERB BUTTER

If you didn't already know it, I'm here to tell you butter makes everything better. Yes, that includes steak! Don't believe me? Once you make this flavorful butter, cut off a piece, and place it on top of your next steak while it rests to melt all over the crust. After that first bite—you will be converted. If you love it, you can also make a double batch and lather it onto your steak before grilling for extra flavor and crispness. And don't limit yourself to steak. This butter is also great on eggs, pork chops, and salmon.

PREP TIME: 15 MINUTES, PLUS 30 MINUTES TO CHILL

Makes about 1½ cups (about 350 g)

1½ cups (336 g) unsalted butter, at room temperature

2 tablespoons (8 g) chopped fresh parsley

2 tablespoons (2 g) chopped fresh cilantro

2 teaspoons chopped fresh chives

2 teaspoons fresh lemon juice

2 teaspoons sea salt

1 teaspoon red pepper flakes

1. In a medium-size food-safe bowl, combine the butter and remaining ingredients. Stir together to mix well.

2. Place a 1-foot (30 cm)-long piece of parchment paper on a work surface. Place the herb butter at one side of the paper and begin to roll it into a log, rolling it tightly. Twist and secure the ends. Refrigerate to set for 30 minutes. Keep any leftovers refrigerated in an airtight container for up to 3 days.

Herb Butter Variations

Besides bacon, I think butter is the other ingredient that makes everything taste better. (There's a reason steakhouses use it to make their steak even more delicious!) If my Steakhouse Butter caught your eye, here are a few variations to try. Use the ingredients in the variations that follow with the instructions on page 186. Your next steak night is sure to be a hit.

Garlic Parmesan Butter: In a small bowl, stir together 1½ cups (336 g) unsalted butter, at room temperature, 1½ tablespoons (6 g) chopped fresh parsley, 1 tablespoon (2.5 g) chopped fresh basil, 1 tablespoon (5 g) shredded Parmesan, 2 teaspoons minced garlic, 1 teaspoon fresh lemon juice, and 1 teaspoon sea salt.

Buffalo and Blue Cheese Butter: In a small bowl, stir together 1½ cups (336 g) unsalted butter, at room temperature, 2 tablespoons (6 g) chopped fresh chives, 1½ tablespoons (12 g) crumbled blue cheese, 2 teaspoons buffalo hot sauce, and 1 teaspoon sea salt.

Hatch Chili-Lime Butter: In a small bowl, stir together 1½ cups (336 g) unsalted butter, at room temperature, 2 tablespoons (2 g) chopped fresh cilantro, 1½ tablespoons (13.5 g) finely chopped Hatch chili, 2 teaspoons fresh lime juice, 1 teaspoon grated lime zest, and 1 teaspoon sea salt.

Lemon-Dill Butter: In a small bowl, stir together 1½ cups (336 g) unsalted butter, at room temperature, 1½ tablespoons (6 g) chopped fresh dill, 2 teaspoons fresh lemon juice, 1½ teaspoons minced garlic, 1 teaspoon lemon zest, and 1 teaspoon sea salt

Chilean Pebre Butter: In a small bowl, stir together 1½ cups (336 g) unsalted butter, at room temperature, 1 diced Roma tomato, 1 tablespoon (4 g) chopped fresh parsley, 1 tablespoon (6 g) diced fresh scallions, 2 teaspoons minced garlic, 1 teaspoon diced serrano peppers, and 1 teaspoon sea salt

Maple Brown Sugar Cinnamon Butter: In a small bowl, stir together 1½ cups (336 g) unsalted butter, at room temperature, 1 tablespoon (15 g) brown sugar, 2 teaspoons cinnamon, 2 teaspoons maple syrup, and 1 teaspoon sea salt

LEMON-CHILI MARINADE

If you are looking to spice up your food with a little citrus and heat, this lemon-chili marinade is the ticket. Inspired by the peri peri flavors I experienced in South Africa, this delicious marinade gives an excellent depth of flavor to beef, chicken, pork, or seafood. My favorite way to use this is to marinate chicken thighs or skirt steak overnight. Grill the meat over direct heat until it's done and you are in business.

PREP TIME: 10 MINUTES

Makes 1 cup (240 ml)

4 or 5 garlic cloves, finely chopped

2 habanero peppers, finely chopped

2 tablespoons (2 g) chopped fresh cilantro

2 tablespoons (30 ml) white vinegar

1 tablespoon (18 g) kosher salt

1 tablespoon (7.5 g) chipotle powder

1 tablespoon (3 g) dried oregano

Juice of 1 lemon

Grated zest of 1 lemon

1. In a medium-size food-safe bowl, stir together the marinade thoroughly. Refrigerate any leftover marinade in an airtight container for up to 3 days.

CHIPOTLE RUB

Need some spiciness in your life? This rub is the ticket! While the chipotle packs a punch, this rub also has tons of savory flavor coming from the cumin and onion. Use this seasoning on seafood, steak, pork, or fruit. It is a great rub to have in your back pocket (not literally . . . although I won't judge) anytime you need to impress guests with your cooking.

PREP TIME: 5 MINUTES

Makes ½ cup (about 72 g)

2 tablespoons (36 g) kosher salt

1 tablespoon (6 g) black pepper

1 tablespoon (9 g) garlic powder

2 teaspoons chipotle powder

2 teaspoons ground cumin

1 teaspoon ancho chili powder

1 teaspoon dried parsley flakes

1 teaspoon onion powder

1. In a small food-safe bowl, stir together all the rub ingredients thoroughly. Store in an airtight container in your cabinet for up to 6 months.

Know your Salt

Even something seemingly simple, like the difference between fine salt versus coarse-grained salt, can make a difference in the results when you cook over fire.

x **Table salt**: This is the classic salt you find at the grocery store, or at restaurants in little saltshakers. Table salt is finely ground, widely available, and perfectly okay to use when cooking over fire.

x **Kosher salt**: The big brother to classic table salt, kosher salt is coarsely ground, making it easier to see when you sprinkle it over meat. It is also widely available and versatile.

x **Sea salt**: This is my favorite type of salt to use on steak. Harvested from salty seawater, containing numerous other minerals, I find that sea salt, finely ground or coarse, lends additional flavor to food versus table salt. I recommend using sea salt for specific cuts, such as New York strip and rib eye, or lightly sprinkling it on foods to finish at the end of the cook.

x **Other salts**: There are many other salts available for cooking, including Himalayan pink salt and Celtic salt. Each has a different flavor profile and unique color.

BEER BASTING BRINE

Basting is a key technique for transferring flavor to food while it cooks. The moisture the baste imparts to the meat is what keeps it delicious, tender, and succulent. Larger cuts of meat require a big-boy basting sauce—introducing the Beer Basting Brine designed to conquer any cut of meat you cook by, near, or over the fire. Lightly mix this brine next to the fire and you are in for a long cook of Hanging Chicken (page 104), Whole Lamb al Asador (page 109), Rotisserie Leg of Lamb (page 130), and more.

PREP TIME: 10 MINUTES | COOK TIME: 15 MINUTES

Makes 5 cups ([1.2 L]; enough for about 3 hours of basting on most recipes)

3 (12-ounce, or 260 ml) bottles of your favorite beer

1 white onion, cubed

2 lemons, halved

2 bay leaves

12 garlic cloves, unpeeled

1 cup (240 ml) white wine vinegar

¼ cup (60 ml) olive oil

2 tablespoons (36 g) kosher salt

2 tablespoons (11.2 g) red pepper flakes

1. Preheat your fire using the instructions for the Skillet method (see page 30), bringing it to a medium temperature (about 300°F, or 150°C).

2. In a cast-iron skillet, combine all basting brine ingredients and place the skillet over the fire. Bring to a simmer and cook for 10 minutes to blend the flavors. Transfer to a cooler spot over the fire to simmer on low heat. Using a basting brush, herb brush, or mop, baste your meat while it cooks. Discard any leftover brine.

SIMPLE BARBECUE SEASONING

True, you would need a library of delicious seasonings to truly do barbecue justice. Although I can't do the impossible and offer that, I do have this delicious time-tested mixture to offer. This seasoning goes on just about anything—from pork shoulder and beef chuck roast to fish and even pork belly. While it might not sum up *all* the flavors of barbecue, it will help you achieve delicious sweet and savory notes when cooking over fire. Just add a little smoke and you are good to go.

PREP TIME: 5 MINUTES

Makes ½ cup (about 72 g)

1½ tablespoons (23 g) light brown sugar

1 tablespoon (8.4 g) smoked paprika

1 tablespoon (6.9 g) onion powder

1 tablespoon (18 g) kosher salt

1 tablespoon (6 g) black pepper

1 teaspoon ground cinnamon

1. In a small food-safe bowl, stir together all the rub ingredients thoroughly. Store in an airtight container in your cabinet for up to 6 months.

MAPLE-BOURBON GLAZE

If you have not figured it out already, I *really* love bourbon. Not only do I love it enough to collect it, but I enjoy cooking with it as well. This glaze was one the first recipes I made when I first fell in love with bourbon's flavor. While there are only three ingredients, it packs a massive flavor punch. Just make sure you cook off some of the alcohol from the bourbon to get a nice smooth flavor. I recommend keeping the glaze over a slightly cooler part of the grill as it can burn if it gets too hot. Try this glaze on chicken wings, pork chops, ribs, or smoked salmon.

PREP TIME: 10 MINUTES | COOK TIME: 5 MINUTES

Makes about ½ cup (120 ml)

¼ cup (60 ml) bourbon

¼ cup (80 g) maple syrup

2 tablespoons (28 g) unsalted butter

FOR SPECIAL GEAR

Basting skillet

Basting brush

1. Preheat your fire using the instructions for the Skillet method (see page 30), bringing it to a medium temperature (about 300°F, or 150°C).

2. Preheat a basting skillet over direct heat. Carefully pour the bourbon into the skillet. Let it simmer for 2 to 3 minutes. Pull the skillet off direct heat and add the maple syrup and butter. Stir until smooth.

3. Once done glazing your meat, pull it off the grill and serve the remaining glaze on the side for added flavor.

GARLIC ONION MARINADE

This marinade has been one of my go-to recipes for years. The onion flavor mixes so well with the mustard, red wine vinegar, and seasonings. Use it for flank steak, lamb, pork kebabs, skirt steak, whole chicken, and more for some epic cooking. Before pouring the marinade over the meat, save some to baste with while cooking. You will thank me later.

PREP TIME: 10 MINUTES

Makes 1½ cups (360 ml)

1 white onion, cubed

15 garlic cloves, peeled

2 tablespoons (30 g) Dijon mustard

2 tablespoons (30 ml) red wine vinegar

1 tablespoon (3 g) dried oregano

1 tablespoon (7 g) ground cumin

1 tablespoon (15 ml) hot sauce

2 teaspoons smoked paprika

2 teaspoons black pepper

2 teaspoons sea salt

1. In a food processor, combine all the marinade ingredients. Blend thoroughly until smooth. Any unused marinade can be refrigerated in an airtight container for up to 3 days.

RESOURCES

GEAR, MATERIALS, AND MORE

Spices and Meat

Spiceology + Derek Wolf (spiceology.com)
For years, I have had the pleasure of creating a few different lines of seasonings and rubs with Spiceology. Inspired by my travels and flavors I remember from childhood, the team at Spiceology helped me create multiple lines from American Inspired to Beer Infused BBQ. If you love my recipes, these spices are an amazing next step!
Recommended: Chipotle Garlic, Gaucho Steakhouse, and Hickory Peach Porter

Porter Road Butchers (porterroad.com)
Chris and James created Porter Road Butcher in my hometown Nashville, TN awhile back. What started as a local butcher shop dedicated to providing high quality local meat has turned into an online meat empire. These two are now able to ship their amazing products all over the country, including my favorite picanha. Although they are now a larger business, I still love shopping at their store in East Nashville.
Recommended: Picanha, Flap Steak, and Hanger Steak

Grills, Skillets, and Wood

Breeo (breeo.co)
Breeo is an American-made smokeless grill that I have been using for years. It creates an amazing cooking experience that provides consistent heat for all direct styles of fire cooking. This has been my daily grill for a while!
Recommended: X Series and The Outpost

Oklahoma Joe's Smokers (oklahomajoes.com)
If you are looking for a top-notch smoker, then look no further than Oklahoma Joe's. They have many options for smokers that you can use for both direct and indirect styles of fire cooking. They also have a starter smoker for those wanting to venture into barbecue.
Recommended: Highland and the Bronco

Cowboy Charcoal (cowboycharcoal.com)
The team at Cowboy Charcoal/Western BBQ Wood/Duraflame are on a mission to make quality charcoal and wood affordable. I love their lump charcoal as it is so easy to light, keeps a lasting heat, and creates an amazing aroma. Pairing it with some of their wood chips or wood chunks is just the cherry on top of a great cook.
Recommended: Oak and Hickory Natural Lump Charcoal and the Mesquite Wood Chips

Kankay Amara (kankaytexas.com)
This little South American based grilling company makes some simple and approachable fire cooking devices. I have fallen in love with how easy they are to light up, as well as the variety of cooking styles you can try on them.
Recommended: Kankay Amara Grill 2.0

Lodge Cast Iron (lodgemfg.com)

If you are looking for a variety of cast iron products as well as fire cooking gear, then look no further than Lodge Cast Iron. With their foundry only a little ways from where I live, they are a local Tennessee business with a large following. I used their cast iron skillets, sauce melting skillet, basting brush, and tri-pod in this cookbook. Look through their site, and you will find many fun cooking apparatuses to try.

Recommended: 12" Cast Iron Skillet, Melting Skillet & Dutch Oven Tri-Pod

Specialty Fire Cooking Equipment

Super Skewers (superskewer.com)

These are the only skewers that I use over the fire. They are high quality, large enough to handle a lot of meat, and easy to clean. There are plenty of options to choose from, which means you're sure to find what you need for your cooking style.

Recommended: Brazilian Churrasco Skewer and Forked Skewer

Kanka Grills (kankagrill.com)

If you are looking for an epic rotisserie, the Kanka rotisserie is perfect. It is packable, lightweight, and super powerful. You can see it in this book on my Rotisserie Leg of Lamb recipe, but it can hold even more weight if you need it to. This is an excellent rotisserie that you can use with just about any grill.

Recommended: The Kanka Grill Rotisserie

Zoro (zoro.com)

This has been one of my favorite places to find interesting and unique fire cooking equipment. For those that are looking for the Food Grade Stainless Steel Shovel, here is the place to snag one.

Recommended: Food Grade Stainless Steel Shovel

Titan Great Outdoors (titangreatoutdoors.com)

Another local Nashville company, Titan Great Outdoors is the place that I got my Asado Cross. It is durable and affordable piece of equipment that any fire cook should have in their arsenal.

Recommended: Asado Cross with Adjustable Base

Knives & Cutting Boards

Fingal Ferguson (fingalfergusonknives.com)

The mad Irishman behind my favorite knives is none other than Fingal Ferguson. He makes some of the most beautiful knives on the planet! I highly recommend grabbing some (if you can find one before it sells out)!

Recommended: Anything!

Monnier Woodcraft

Monnier Woodcraft have been the only cutting boards that I have used for years. They are durable and super high quality. Made in Texas, buying one also means supporting American artists.

Recommended: Any end grain cutting board.

ACKNOWLEDGMENTS

———

The list of people who have helped me along this journey is endless. I will do my best to thank everyone who has been an inspiration to *Over The Fire Cooking* and its growth.

I, first, want to thank Jesus who has blessed me beyond measure. I have made my fair share of mistakes during these past few years, but He has always given me grace and mercy. I could not have done this without Him.

To my wife, Ally: Thank you for the endless days of putting up with me learning how to cook, burning things, and starting all over. You have been my rock through these years and have shown me what it means to be consistent, loving, and full of grace. I love you more than words can express.

To my family and friends, thank you for always volunteering and helping! My parents, Brad and Denise, you built the foundation of this journey. I owe you everything—and then some. My sister and brother-in-law, Jenna and Evan, you have always been willing to provide support when needed and to eat all the leftovers. You guys give Ally and me faith in the future. To the Klinkers: Thank you so much for showing me what it means to push things to the limit and dream big. You inspire Ally and me to keep going for it every day! To Drew, Erin, Anthony, and Haley: You have always been willing to help in any way possible whenever needed—whether that is cooking, cleaning, or going on insane adventures. Thank you for being such amazing friends.

To those who inspired me, thank you for investing in *Over The Fire Cooking*. Friends like Christie Vanover, Matt Crawford, and Pete Taylor, you have made me a better cook, friend, and person. I am excited to see what the future holds for you. To those willing to be featured on my page in the beginning, I would not have learned or developed without you. You are a part of *Over The Fire Cooking* as much as anyone!

Lastly, to my followers: Thank you for being so encouraging and caring. Whether you have followed the whole time or just a little, you make a difference. Thank you for your time, questions, investment, and engagement. You are the biggest reason we can do this!

ABOUT THE AUTHOR

Derek Wolf is the man behind Over The Fire Cooking: a website, video, and social media phenomenon dedicated to bringing fire, food, and people together. In addition to his original recipes and videos, Derek builds community on his pages by featuring the adventures of other fire-cooking enthusiasts. Derek frequently travels around the world to learn new techniques and recipes, works with various brands from Cowboy Charcoal to Oklahoma Joe's, and has multiple bestselling spice lines with Spiceology. He has been featured everywhere from *Forbes* to *Southern Cast Iron* magazine, made TV shorts with Buffalo Trace, and loves cooking for large crowds at festivals. Most weeks you can still find him working on new recipes, producing and showcasing them on his website and socials. Check out more of his work on Instagram, Facebook, YouTube, and more at @OverTheFireCooking or visit him at OverTheFireCooking.com.

INDEX